MEMORY POWER-UP

101 WAYS TO INSTANT RECALL

"Many complain of their memory, few of their judgment."

MEMORY POWER-UP

101 WAYS TO INSTANT RECALL

MICHAEL TIPPER

DUNCAN BAIRD PUBLISHERS

LONDON

MEMORY POWER-UP

Michael Tipper

Author's dedication: Mom, this one is for you.

Distributed in the USA and Canada by Sterling Publishing Co., Inc.
387 Park Avenue South, New York, NY 10016-8810

This edition first published in the UK and USA in 2007 by
Duncan Baird Publishers Ltd
Sixth Floor, Castle House, 75–76 Wells Street, London W1T 3QH

Managing Editor: Caroline Ball
Editor: Daphne Razazan
Assistant Editor: Kirty Topiwala
Managing Designer: Clare Thorpe
Commissioned illustrations: Bonnie Dain for Lilla Rogers Studio and 3+Co.

Library of Congress Cataloging-in-Publication Data Available
ISBN-13: 978-1-84483-410-5   ISBN-10: 1-84483-410-7

10 9 8 7 6 5 4 3 2 1

Typeset in Trade Gothic
Color reproduction by Scanhouse, Malaysia
Printed and bound in Singapore

For information about custom editions, special sales, premium and corporate
purchases, please contact Sterling Special Sales Department at 800-805-5489
or specialsales@sterlingpub.com.

Mind Map® is a registered trademark of The Buzan Organisation Limited 1990

CONTENTS

"The secret of a good memory is attention, and attention to a subject depends upon our interest in it. We rarely forget that which has made a deep impression on our minds."

Tryon Edwards (1809–94)

INTRODUCTION

Many people think that they have a bad memory, and if you've picked up this book, I'm guessing that you do, too. I know exactly how you feel, because some years ago I thought exactly the same and, just as you are now, I began searching for answers to solve what I thought was my "problem".

At the time I was just 16 years old and had joined the Royal Navy as a naval apprentice, eager to learn my new trade. Although I'd done reasonably well at school, I soon discovered that the Navy was a very different learning environment from the classroom, and I began to struggle, especially with having to remember so much new information so quickly. I naturally assumed my memory was at fault and sought ways to improve it. I soon discovered, though, that nothing was wrong with my memory: I just didn't know how to use it.

I found a memory course advertised in a newspaper, very quickly mastered some simple techniques, and began passing my exams with ease. With my new skills, I quickly impressed my superiors and was selected for officer training. I then went on to complete a degree in engineering and subsequently joined the Royal Navy's élite Submarine Service.

My later naval training tested my memory and learning skills even further, and I regularly came top of most of the courses I attended, even when my fellow students were more talented and able than myself. The only difference between us was that I had equipped myself with better learning strategies.

Eventually, I found myself telling more and more of my colleagues and friends about how to improve their memory and learning skills, and discovered a passion and a talent for sharing these ideas and helping people develop. At about the same time I entered the World Memory Championships; at my second attempt I won the Silver Medal and became a Grand Master of Memory.

My success led to a professional speaking career, and over the last few years I've personally worked with over 65,000 people all over the world and have developed programmes that have been taught to over half a million people.

From my own experience and from all the work I've done with countless people over the years, I know that you can improve your memory by understanding how it works and by discovering some basic ideas that anyone can apply. This book has captured all of the most powerful strategies I've used, and helped others use to great effect to get more from their memory and improve their recall.

Decide for yourself whether you need this book by reading the statements opposite. Simply answer "yes", "no" or "sometimes". If you answer "yes" or "sometimes" to five or more of these statements, this book will definitely help you. Even though you might think you have a problem with your memory, I'm delighted to tell you that you probably don't. The only thing that's wrong is that you don't know how to use it because I doubt whether anyone ever taught you.

This book will take you step by step through some simple techniques and strategies (the "how") that will not only improve your memory but also your levels of concentration and mental agility.

DO THESE APPLY TO YOU?

- I have difficulty remembering the names of people I've just met.
- I have difficulty remembering the names of people I met longer than a few weeks ago.
- I often walk into a room to get something and can't remember what it is.
- I often forget where I've left my keys/purse/glasses.
- I have on occasion parked the car and been unable to find it.
- I regularly miss important appointments because I've forgotten about them.
- I'm well known for missing friends' and relatives' birthdays and anniversaries.
- I have to write down the PIN number to my ATM card.
- If I lost my cellphone and had to call the service provider, I'd have no idea what number to ring.
- I always avoid standing up and talking to groups of people because I know I'm going to forget what I have to say.
- I spend hours reading all sorts of material and can hardly remember anything about what I've read.
- I think that, as I'm getting older, my memory is getting worse.
- I find myself saying things like "I have a terrible memory" or "I always forget."
- I almost expect to forget something that I was supposed to remember.
- I'd like to learn something new but don't think my memory is up to it.

CHAPTER 1

WARM-UPS

You'll develop extremely powerful recall when you follow the simple techniques in this book. However, before you embark on them, it will help if you understand some of the reasons why your memory might appear to you to be unsatisfactory, together with some of the basics that will form the foundation of your memory improvement skills.

This chapter will look at why people like you forget, showing you that this is not necessarily because you're getting older. I'll tell you a little bit about the brain and how you file away and recall your memories, as well as about the key principles of a strong memory. I'll also give you a five-step plan that, if followed, will guarantee your success in improving your memory.

WHY DO WE FORGET?

Before we look at what you can do to enhance your memory, it's useful to realize why we forget. The factors that affect our ability to recall are related to the information we're receiving, the mental and physical state we're in both at the time and afterwards, and some of the processes that naturally occur in the brain.

COMMON REASONS FOR FORGETTING

There are various causes of forgetfulness, which can affect us all at different times:

- **Not interested** – if you're not interested in something, it's unlikely you'll pay any attention to it. As a result, you won't be able to understand, learn about or remember it.
- **Not concentrating** – this is linked to not being interested. If something doesn't capture your attention, you won't concentrate on it. If you're not concentrating and are thinking about something else, you won't take the new information in, however crucial it might be to remember it.
- **Too stressed** – when you're stressed you're in the worst possible state to use your memory effectively. It's either hard to learn things or difficult to recall them.
- **Too much information** – if you're faced with a barrage of information, it's easy to become overwhelmed (and therefore stressed), making it hard to learn and remember.

- **Poorly organized information** – it's much harder to remember random bits of data than it is to recall information that has been logically organized.
- **Weak links** – as we'll see later, the brain remembers things by association. If the links between related pieces of information are weak (for example, between a name and a face), recall will be difficult. If you don't use the information you've learnt, it won't integrate with your existing knowledge, which will also result in weak links and poor recall.
- **Too long ago** – if a long period of time has elapsed between encountering something and having to recall it, the memory of it will be much weaker.
- **Interference** – with so much information coming to your mind, there's a strong possibility that the new data will interfere with your existing knowledge and that the new information in turn will be interfered with by newer data as that arrives, which will adversely affect your recall.

Fortunately, by making some simple changes to the way that we think, we can easily overcome these common causes of forgetfulness and improve our memory capacity enormously.

"Pleasure is the flower that passes;
remembrance, the lasting perfume."

Jean de Boufflers (1738–1815)

IS IT MY AGE?

As people get older, many start to experience challenges with their memory and naturally assume the decline in their mental performance is due to their age. However, unless you're suffering from a disease or illness, your memory doesn't necessarily deteriorate with time.

YOUR MEMORY DOESN'T HAVE TO DECLINE

Studies with people over 60 have shown little or no deterioration in memory performance – only a slightly slower reaction time. The apparent decline that so many people expect to happen is often caused by a combination of the following factors:

- Older people don't use their memory as much as they used to.
- Their brain isn't getting as much oxygen as it did when they were younger, because they're probably getting less exercise.
- They've generated a belief that they have a declining memory because of forgetting one or two things. They strengthen this belief by telling themselves and others that they have a poor memory.
- By being less in the present, they often miss things and then blame their memory because they can't remember, whereas in fact it's their concentration that's at fault.

All these factors can be reversed by making some lifestyle changes as well as adapting the way you think, so that you can have a good memory however old you are.

YOUR MENTAL FILING SYSTEM

If your memory isn't performing as you'd like it to, you may not be organizing information in a way that enables you to recall it easily. It's simply a question of tuning your already powerful memory retrieval system.

YOU THINK LIKE A VIRTUAL FILING CABINET

Imagine your memory is a huge virtual filing cabinet. For example, at a business meeting you're introduced to someone called David Jones. You store his face and name in a mental file marked **"met David Jones at business meeting"**.

In future when you see a face you recognize, you go to your mental filing system to the file where that face is stored. This file tells you the face belongs to someone called David Jones.

SEE FACE > MENTAL FILE > RETRIEVE NAME

Or you may hear the name David Jones and in your mental filing system the file with that name on it shows you a picture of him.

HEAR NAME > MENTAL FILE > RETRIEVE FACE

EXERCISE 1

Read the two words at the top of the next page, noting exactly what you think and how long it takes to formulate your thoughts.

HILLARY CLINTON

Most people who do this exercise instantly see a picture of Hillary Clinton in their mind's eye. It might be an image of her face from one of her many TV appearances or from a mini-movie of her giving a speech. Or it could be a shot of her with her husband on the cover of a glossy magazine.

The exact image that first comes to mind will depend on your own personal associations with Hillary Clinton. It doesn't matter what picture you see, because, whichever one you're most familiar with, this exercise demonstrates how powerful your mental retrieval system is.

In literally an instant you were able to go straight to an image of Hillary Clinton and retrieve it. Instantaneously you found it from among the many millions and millions of unique images that you've stored in your brain. That's an incredible feat of recall and one you should be proud of.

EXERCISE 2

Now try a variation on this exercise by listening to the news on the radio, and noticing just how quickly pictures come into your mind of the people, topics or places that the newsreader is talking about. Once again, the speed at which you'll find you can evoke vivid, appropriate images should reassure you of just how strong your powers of memory already are.

EXERCISE 3

Repeat the Hillary Clinton exercise with a friend and compare
their image with yours, noticing just how unique your pictures and
associations are.

THE POWER OF ASSOCIATION

The process by which you can conjure up images of Hillary Clinton
and other people and topics on the news is known as association. And
it's this process that enables you to go to your mental filing cabinet to
find and swiftly retrieve the name or face of David Jones, or whoever
you've been introduced to.

The mind organizes associations in a combination of two ways.
First, it organizes them as a chain so that one thing will remind us
of another, which prompts us to think of something else, and this in
turn triggers a further memory, and so on. Second, it groups them as
a series of hooks – one concept will have a series of associations all
directly linked to the original idea.

By understanding this, you can harness your mind more effectively
to create powerful associations that will help you remember and recall
far more than you can at present. And you will find that your ability to
instantly summon up your associations is staggering.

"Everyone has a photographic memory.
Some just don't have any film."

Anonymous

YOUR BRAIN AND YOUR MEMORY

Your brain is the control centre of everything that happens in your body. Every second there are thousands of chemical and electrical reactions taking place in the grey matter between your ears. When you understand how your brain functions a little better, you'll be able to use it more effectively to improve your memory.

THE BUILDING BLOCKS

The brain is made up of billions of cells called neurons, and each of these is capable of connecting with thousands of other neurons. The complexity and sheer scale of the number of these connections give the brain its near-infinite potential. Every thought you've experienced, every sensation you've felt and every memory you've ever had is a connection between two or more of these neurons.

The brain in cross-section

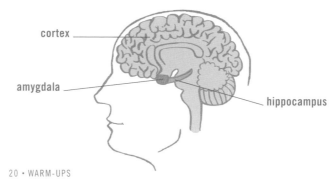

cortex

amygdala

hippocampus

THE BIGGER PIECES

To explain the functioning of such a complex and interconnected mechanism as the brain is impossible in a few words. However, there are a few "big pieces" you should be aware of when considering your memory.

The **amygdala** tags incoming information with emotional value. The more emotionally charged an experience, the more likely it is to be remembered.

The **hippocampus** is responsible for the transference of short-term memories into the long term. It's also the part of the brain that "lights up" when we think about something or somewhere we know well (something we'll take advantage of later in this book).

The **cortex** is sometimes known as the thinking part of the brain, because this is where our conscious thought processes take place. It consists of two halves, and research done over 40 years ago identified different functions for each half. It was thought that the distinction between the two areas was simply this:

LEFT SIDE	RIGHT SIDE
Lists, Lines, Logic, Words, Number, Order	Rhythm, Colour, Spatial awareness, Pictures, Daydreaming, Imagination

It's now known that the relationship between the two halves of the brain is much more complex, and the current theory is that the left brain processes in a more serial manner and the right brain in a more parallel manner. Or, to put it another way, research has demonstrated that the left brain focuses on the detail, whereas the right brain sees the bigger picture.

Traditional ways of learning and remembering have focused on the activities associated with the left brain functions. What's now certain is that the more you use both sides of the brain, the more effective your thinking will be and the better your memory.

DIFFERENT FREQUENCIES

At different levels of consciousness ranging from the wide awake state to that of deep sleep, the brain exhibits electrical activity at different frequencies.

The beta (β) frequencies are the highest, and dominate when we're wide awake. The alpha frequencies (α) become more prevalent at the relaxed but alert state. As we drift into a deeper meditative state on the way to falling asleep, we encounter more theta (θ) waves, and finally, once we're in a deep sleep, the delta (δ) frequencies take over.

Learning is most effective in the alpha state when we're calm and relaxed. Fortunately, we're able to access this state using meditation and relaxation techniques as a way of enhancing memory.

WHAT AFFECTS YOUR BRAIN WILL AFFECT YOUR MEMORY

As a delicate and finely tuned instrument, your brain will be affected by a variety of factors that are within your control. Excess caffeine, nicotine and alcohol upset the delicate chemical balance within the brain, which undoubtedly impairs its performance. What you eat also has an effect, and a healthy balanced diet will help in improving your mental performance. Eating specific memory-enhancing foods can also be beneficial, particularly those, such as citrus and berry fruits and leafy green vegetables, that are rich in antioxidants (see p.41).

OXYGEN AND THE BRAIN

Without sufficient oxygen, your brain (and then you) will die. The importance of oxygen is clear when you consider that the brain might be only two percent of the body's weight but consumes over 25 percent of its oxygen intake. The more efficient your ability to breathe well, the more oxygen will get to your brain, which is one of the reasons that exercise is so important, as we'll see later.

THE IMPORTANCE OF SLEEP

Sleep is not only vital to the healthy functioning of your brain, but also crucial for learning and memory. Numerous studies have shown that people remember more effectively if they have a good night's sleep after learning. It's believed that during sleep the brain revisits its recent experiences to reinforce them and etch them into the memory. Contrary to popular belief, new learning doesn't take place while we're asleep, only the integration of information already learnt.

"Memory … is the diary that we all carry about with us."

Oscar Wilde (1854–1900)

IMAGINATION, ASSOCIATION AND RECALL

Your brain is like an amazing computer that sadly doesn't come with a user manual. You began learning how to use it by trial and error and slowly developed the thinking skills you now have. There are ways in which you can build on those and use your mind to improve your ability to remember.

ACHIEVE MORE BY DOING LESS!

It's a common misconception that the harder and longer you work at learning something, the more likely you are to be able to remember it. Fortunately, this isn't true because our minds don't naturally work like that. When you're engaged in a learning task, you're more likely to recall information from the beginning and end of the session, with a dip in your memory of the topics from the middle.

This is called the Primacy and Recency Effect. The longer the period of time you work, the bigger the dip and the less you'll recall. The secret is to take more breaks so you have more primacy and recency "high points" of recall. A good rule of thumb is to work for between 20 and 50 minutes and then take a five- to 10-minute break. Not only will you remember more, but you'll stay fresh and alert longer.

THE SECRET OF HAVING A POWERFUL MEMORY

There are three simple stages for developing your memory to its full potential. Here's the secret of being able to remember absolutely anything you want to for as long as you want to:

HOW TO USE YOUR IMAGINATION

Think about the last time you walked down a street full of people. Is there anyone who particularly stood out? You might have walked past hundreds of people yet can't remember any of them. However, if a seven-foot-tall woman wearing a bright yellow coat, red hat with bright blue feathers and black leather boots, had ridden past on a pink elephant, singing the national anthem, do you think you might have remembered her? Of course you would, because that image would have stood out from all the other people you saw.

Not everything in our lives is as unique and outstanding, but with the power of our imaginations we can make anything as memorable as we want by applying a few simple principles.

Here are just a few ways to add some "memory spice":

- Think in pictures and symbols even for dry and boring subjects.
- Use lots of vibrant and striking colours.
- Exaggerate by making small things large.

"Imagination is more powerful than knowledge."

Albert Einstein (1879–1955)

- Distort by making large things small.
- Create pictures with lots of movement.
- Use and engage all your senses.
- Be as outrageous as you can by making the images crude and shocking.
- Use bizarre and unusual associations.
- Make things as funny as possible – a touch of humour can make them particularly memorable.

The easiest way to describe this process in one sentence is for you to start thinking like a Tom and Jerry cartoon! Don't worry, you don't have to be a budding animator – just give your imagination free rein. You may be surprised at what you come up with.

ASSOCIATION – THE KEY TO EFFECTIVE RECALL

We saw earlier that the brain is an associative mechanism in that it organizes its memories by association. There are two ways in which it does so. The first is by a sequence or chain of associations – one thing will trigger another, which itself will prompt a third thing, and so on. For example:

TREE > PARK > WALK > FEET > SHOES > LACES

The other way is by a collection of associations or hooks. One idea or concept will have a series of related words linked to it, as in the beach example opposite.

By creating strong chains between items you want to remember and by using multiple hooks, you'll be able to recall things much more effectively, especially if you enhance those links by using your imagination in the way that I've described above.

ORGANIZING YOUR ASSOCIATIONS

Having a series of strong associations will serve you well only if you're able to consciously access them by choice whenever you want to. You now need to organize your powerful filing system of a memory so that it's easy to find any file. The way to do that is to give each file a label. I'll be showing you various labelling methods based on visual techniques. As we've seen with the Hillary Clinton exercise, we tend to think in pictures rather than words or numbers. (Although we've been conditioned over two millennia to think in words, our natural inclination, dating back to the era before written language, is to think in pictures, feelings or sensations.)

REMEMBER FOR LONGER

Many people complain that they can't recall things from the recent past, and they believe this results from a poor memory. What they don't know is that it's normal for this to happen because, within one to two days of encountering new information, you're likely to remember only about 20 percent of it. The reason for this drop-off is the overlaying of similar or related information, which makes it harder to distinguish one memory from another, which in turn reduces the ability to recall. This is known as the **confusion** factor. Rather than arising from a poor memory, the inability to remember the new information is the result of not having a proper and effective process to condition the recall so that you'll *always* be able to recapture it.

REHEARSE THE RECALL

If you really want to remember something important, you need to practise recalling it from memory after 10 minutes, a day, a week, a month, three months and six months. After that it will be in your long-term memory and you'll always be able to recall it because you'll have conditioned it into your mind.

BREAK IT DOWN INTO LITTLE PIECES

Think of the children's joke, "How do you eat an elephant?," to which the answer is, "One bite at a time." The same principle applies when dealing with things that you have to remember. Breaking things down into smaller, more manageable chunks makes remembering them much easier.

In this book I'll give you specific and powerful ways to use imagination, association and recall to organize your mental files so you can access them easily and recall what you've memorized.

GUIDING
PRINCIPLES

Here are the general principles that will apply to everything you'll learn about improving your memory in the rest of the book.

* * * * *

Work for 20–50 minutes and take five- to 10-minute breaks.

* * *

Use your imagination to create strong, memorable images that stand out in your mind.

* * *

Create powerful associations using hooks and chains.

* * *

Organize your associations by using one of the many mental filing systems that you'll learn about in this book.

* * *

Regularly rehearse recalling what you've learned to ensure long-term recall.

* * *

Break things down into smaller, more manageable chunks.

"I've a grand memory for forgetting."

Robert Louis Stevenson (1850–94)

BEING CERTAIN OF SUCCESS

If you look at people who've achieved anything of note in any area of their lives, there are some common things they'll have done to ensure success. Whether you want to climb the highest mountain, find a new job or improve your memory, you're more likely to reach your goal if you have the mindset of a successful person.

FIVE STEPS TO SUCCESS
Step 1 – Have a goal

This is the most important step, because if you don't have a clearly defined target you'll never know if you've hit it. Your goal needs to be easy to understand, measurable, have a deadline and be **written down**. Writing it down is essential because it's the first step as your goal translates from a fleeting idea inside your mind into reality.

Here are two examples of written goals:

- I want to improve my memory.
- I want to be able to remember straightaway the first and last names of 15 new people I meet at business or social gatherings over the next month and be able to recall their names if I ever meet them again in the future.

The first example is vague with no clear definition of success or when it might be achieved by. The second example is much better because the goal is clearly defined and there's a specific time-frame.

Step 2 – Have a plan

Having set your goal, you now need to make a plan to enable you to achieve it. The simplest approach is to make a list of everything that you need to do to achieve the goal and then organize the list into numbered stages. If we take the goal of wanting to remember names in Step 1, the start of your plan might look like this:

- Read section on remembering names.
- Practise to myself.
- Teach my family the method for remembering names so that I know I understand it.
- Practise on my friends.
- Try out the system with one new person at my next meeting.

Step 3 – Believe you can do it

Not believing you can do something will seriously affect your ability to do it, but fortunately there are two straightforward ways to give your mind the "proof" that you can.

The first is to use self talk (also known as affirmations), which simply involves making positive statements about yourself and your ability. Most people say negative things about themselves, such as:

"I have a poor memory."

or

"I can't remember that."

or

"That's too difficult to learn."

These sorts of statements help to reinforce the belief that you've a poor memory. So instead, to help you improve your memory, you need to say things like:

"I have a fabulous memory."
and
"I always remember the names of everyone I meet."
and
"Learning and remembering new information is easy and fun for me."

The more you repeat these statements, the greater your belief in your powers of memory will become.

A second powerful way to help you with your belief levels is to use your imagination to create little movies in your mind of what it will be like when you're successfully using your great memory. See, hear and feel "perfect memory situations" in great detail and really imagine yourself having the memory ability you desire. Used by the world's top athletes to focus before the big game, this process of imagining a successful outcome is known as "mental rehearsal".

Step 4 – Take action
Now put your plan into action using the stages described in Step 2. Keep going until everything on your list is complete and you've achieved your goal. As you work your way through your plan, check to make sure that your actions are taking you closer to your goal. If not, it's OK to refine and re-write the plan so that it gets you to your

desired outcome more quickly. The key to Step 4 is to keep taking action until the goal is achieved.

Step 5 – Keep a positive attitude

Life has a habit of throwing things in the way as we progress toward our goals, but we're lucky enough to be able to choose how we respond. Letting negative emotions develop when things don't go our way causes stress, which adversely affects how we feel. In terms of developing a good memory, negative emotions are a major barrier to overcome. Keeping a positive outlook on life and reacting to events and circumstances in a positive way won't make problems go away but they'll furnish you with a more resourceful state of mind to deal with them (and it's a lot more fun too!).

To get you started in applying these five simple steps, here are a few exercises:

- Think about all the goals that you have for your memory and write them down so that you know exactly what you want for each one and when you want to achieve it by.
- Choose the most important of your goals and create a plan for achieving it.
- Write down on a card five positive affirmations about attaining this goal, and repeat them to yourself at every opportunity.
- Visualize achieving your goal, using your imagination and all your senses – see it as though it had already happened.
- Start working toward your goal by beginning with the first item on your list of things to do.

CHAPTER 2

GENTLE STRETCHES

Before we start delving into memory improvement techniques, there are, first of all, some straightforward things that you can do in terms of lifestyle that will have a significant effect on your powers of memorization and recall.

This chapter will look at the number one lifestyle challenge to having a correctly functioning memory – the stress factor – and what you can do to overcome it. It will also look at ways to boost your memory faculties through exercise and simple, commonsense changes to your diet, including a guide to memory-enhancing foods. In addition, I'll show you some practical steps you can take immediately to help you recall some of the things that you need to.

MANAGING STRESS FOR A BETTER MEMORY

Stress affects the way we think and in particular the performance of memory. By minimizing the effects of stress, you can create a much better physical and mental environment for your memory, enabling it to perform at its best.

HOW STRESS AFFECTS MEMORY

As we evolved as human beings, our bodies created an effective protection and survival device that was designed to keep us alive when threatened – the fight or flight mechanism.

When faced with a potential danger, we could either tackle it (fight) or run away from it (flight). Whichever choice we made, we needed to breathe faster, produce more adrenaline, tense our muscles and shut down bodily systems that we didn't need.

Today we rarely have to fight or flee. However, we're still bombarded with many things in our personal and professional lives that can be perceived as a threat, and our bodies still respond in the same way, which creates stress.

Stress affects memory in two ways. It shuts down part of the brain responsible for long-term memory, which is why it's difficult to recall information under pressure. Second, if the stress chemicals produced in the brain remain there for longer periods, they create a toxic bath that destroys brain cells, especially those involved in memory.

LEARN TO RELAX

In order to manage stress and help improve your memory, you need to learn to relax. Try some of these exercises to see which work best for you. Do them somewhere quiet where you won't be disturbed.

* * * * *

Physically tense and then consciously relax every muscle in turn, starting from your head and working down to your toes.

* * *

Using your imagination, picture yourself in a peaceful place, such as on a deserted tropical beach or in a secluded meadow, and then imagine the stress and tension draining away from your body.

* * *

Slow your breathing down and count the number of breaths you take in one minute; aim to approximately halve that number for the next minute. Repeat until your breathing rate is slow and deep.

* * *

Practise breath meditation by first physically relaxing every muscle in your body and then focusing on nothing else apart from counting your breaths.

"To the mind that is still, the whole universe surrenders."

Lao Tzu (6th century BC)

EXERCISE TO IMPROVE YOUR MEMORY

A healthy body helps to create a healthy mind, and a good exercise session will not only clear your head but also make you feel better. Exercise also helps to improve memory performance and should be an important part of your memory improvement plan.

EXERCISE HELPS COMBAT STRESS

Regular exercise can overcome the effects of stress in two key ways. First, it provides an outlet for the build-up in the brain of potentially harmful fight or flight chemicals, which can lead to stress. Second, it conditions both the body and the mind to be less susceptible to fatigue and, by doing so, enables them to handle stress more effectively.

DO THE RIGHT EXERCISE

The right kind of exercise to combat stress and improve memory is aerobic – exercise in which your heart rate is 70–85 percent of your maximum (your doctor can advise you on what these rates should be). Exercise at this interim rate for 30 minutes, with a 10-minute warm-up and warm-down, at least three times per week, and preferably five times, in order to obtain maximum benefit.

Brisk walking is a good form of aerobic exercise – try fitting in a fast-paced 30-minute walk in your lunch hour at work. Other ideal aerobic activities are jogging, swimming, cycling and dancing.

WHY DOES AEROBIC EXERCISE IMPROVE MEMORY?

Aerobic exercise is beneficial for the heart, blood vessels and lungs, with the added bonus of helping to improve memory. It generates an increase in the body's need for oxygen – as a result, the heart and lungs have to work a little harder than normal. Heavier breathing during aerobic exercise draws more oxygen into the body, resulting in a faster heart rate. This faster rate pumps the oxygen-enriched blood around the circulatory system. Twenty to 40 percent of this blood flows to the brain and, as the brain thrives on oxygen, it will perform better because of the increased flow.

> ### IT REALLY WORKS!
> Recent research into the effects of exercise on ageing has shown that exercise boosts mental performance generally and in particular improves memory. Additional research into the effects of exercise on academic performance demonstrated that over 80 percent of high-achieving students exercised at least three times per week and that the failure rate of physically fit students was half that of those who were unfit.

START GENTLY

Before you begin an exercise programme, ask your doctor for advice on the most suitable form of exercise for your physical condition and for the all-clear to start. Begin gently – don't rush it. Gradually build up to exercising three times a week for 30 minutes. Try different forms of exercise to discover the one or ones you enjoy the most – you're more likely to stick at them. It also helps to find an exercise buddy to keep you company and, even more critically, keep you motivated.

A BETTER DIET, A BETTER MEMORY

Mental performance and, in particular, memory are affected by what we consume. Consequently, if you choose the right food, you can improve your memory.

A GOOD FOOD FOUNDATION

The foundation for a memory-improving eating plan is a diet that's balanced and healthy – low in fat, salt and sugar, and high in fibre. It should also contain at least five portions of fresh fruit and vegetables a day. A useful rule is to see how "alive and fresh" your food looks.

It's also important to keep the body hydrated. This is because the brain is nearly 80 percent water and if that water level drops through dehydration, the brain's performance will deteriorate.

DEVELOPING A BETTER DIET

To ensure an optimum diet to support your memory-improvement programme, here's what I advise:

- Keep a food journal for a week to monitor what you eat and drink.
- Consult your doctor or a qualified nutritionist for advice on how to adjust your diet to make it healthier, if necessary.
- Eat lots of water-rich foods such as salads and fruits, and drink at least eight glasses of water – three to four pints – a day.
- Eat regularly and maintain your energy levels with "slow-burning" energy foods such as wholewheat bread and pasta, brown rice, wholegrain breakfast cereals, and porridge oats.

- Reduce your intake of salt and sugars, which can be very high in convenience and "junk" food – check the labels carefully.

MEMORY-ENHANCING FOODS

There are also specific foods that enhance memory, notably antioxidants, B vitamins and Omega-3 fatty acids.

ANTIOXIDANTS	B VITAMINS	OMEGA-3 FATTY ACIDS
Alfalfa sprouts	Dairy products	Herring
Berry fruits	Lean meat and	Mackerel
Broccoli	poultry	Salmon
Citrus fruits	Legumes	Sardines
Cranberries	Nuts and seeds	Trout
Grapes	Wheat germ	Tuna (fresh has
Kale		a higher
Mango and papaya		concentration
Spinach		than canned)
Tomatoes		

MEMORY-BOOSTING SUPPLEMENTS

Ginkgo biloba has traditionally been used by Chinese herbalists for a variety of remedies. Scientific studies have shown that extracts stimulate circulation in the brain, which improves short-term memory.

Ginseng helps to neutralize the negative effects of free radicals and excess toxic chemicals in the brain caused by stress.

MEMORY JOGGERS

As you read this book, you'll be able to develop an extremely strong memory and instant recall just by using the power of your mind. However, while you gradually build up your natural memory powers, you shouldn't overlook some simple "artificial" methods that will help you remember a wide spectrum of information.

ARTIFICIAL STORAGE AND RETRIEVAL SYSTEMS

There are a number of practical ways to store information so you can retrieve it whenever you want to, as well as ways to prompt you to remember to do something at exactly the right time. Here are some suggestions.

- Programme your cellphone – set the alarm to remind you of an important appointment or something that you have to do at a specific time.
- Use the refrigerator as a reminder board – write down your list of things to do in large writing on a big piece of paper and stick it on the refrigerator where you'll always see it.
- Keep a journal – reflect on your day by recording in a journal all the significant things that have happened to you and in particular how you feel about them. Remember the journal is private, so record your thoughts and feelings honestly. Reading the journal in a few months' or years' time will assist you in recalling your past and trigger a whole range of associated memories.

- Use your calendar — make a note on your calendar of important dates such as birthdays and anniversaries and when to buy cards and presents.
- Display reminders on your computer — if you use your computer every day, write reminders of things that you have to do on pieces of paper and stick them over your screen so that you'll see them when you log on, or use the reminder software on your computer.
- Bribe your children — if you have young children, prime them to remind you to do something by offering them a little incentive such as ice cream or an extra allowance if they remind you at the right time.

You might think that using these methods is cheating because you're not relying on your natural memory. However, your ability to remember something increases dramatically when you bring that information into the external real world from out of your internal thinking world. When you write something down or type it into an electronic device, you'll see it, feel it and possibly hear it (if you say what it is out loud). All of this will make the information much more memorable.

Try using some of the suggestions I've given you to help in your recall. Or see if you can think of other devices or methods that you could use to help you remember.

"The palest ink is better than the best memory."

Chinese proverb

WHERE DID I LEAVE ...?

Many people, particularly as they get older, start thinking their memory is getting worse because they keep losing their keys, misplacing their purse or even forgetting where they parked the car! They assume a failing memory is responsible for these lapses, but in fact this usually isn't so. A simple technique will ensure you'll never forget where you left your car and never misplace your keys or purse again.

YOUR CONSCIOUS AND SUBCONSCIOUS MIND

In the most basic terms we think on two different levels – consciously and subconsciously.

Your conscious mind is focused at the moment on reading these words on this page. This part of your mind is where you do your conscious thinking as you engage with the world and what's happening around you.

The subconscious deals with everything else not looked after by your conscious mind, and is much larger. For example, your subconscious mind is currently processing the physical sensations being experienced by your left foot, which you weren't aware of until I drew your attention to them.

Your subconscious mind is so powerful that it can allow you to act on "auto-pilot" so you don't even have to think about what you're doing, particularly if it's something you do often, such as taking off your glasses or putting down your house or car keys.

WHY YOU "FORGET" WHERE YOU PUT YOUR KEYS

The reason you misplace items (which you then blame your memory for) is simple. You weren't consciously thinking about them when you put them down, because you were operating on "auto-pilot". You weren't concentrating on what you were doing – in effect, "you" were never "there", which is why you can't consciously remember where you put your keys. Your subconscious will know where they are. However, since we engage with the world through our conscious mind, the keys are as good as lost.

This will inevitably happen more often the older you get, not because your memory is getting worse, but because you will have more memories and associations. As a result, your conscious mind is going to be distracted more often, making it harder to concentrate on what you're doing, especially on mundane everyday activities.

THE SOLUTION IS SIMPLE

In order to be able to remember where you leave something like your purse or keys or even your car, you need to bring its location into your conscious awareness. The easiest way to do this is to say out loud what it is you're putting down or leaving and where you're putting it. For example, "I'm putting my keys on top of the microwave," or "I'm leaving my car on the seventh floor in bay A" – you can say this before you get out of the car to avoid funny looks from other motorists!

Practise describing out loud to yourself where you leave things – whether around the house or when you're out and about – until it becomes a habit.

THAT REMINDS ME ...

If you ever plan to mention something important to a friend or colleague, or maybe do a particular task in the office, and you forget, it can be really frustrating. What you need is a foolproof way to remind you of exactly what to do when you need to do it.

WHY WE FORGET TO DO SOMETHING

There are three main reasons why we sometimes don't remember to do things at the appropriate time:

- When it occurs to us that we need to take some future action, the idea fleetingly passes through our conscious mind and we don't think about it long enough for it to consciously "reappear" at the right time or place.
- Such a lapse in memory occurs mainly when we're doing something habitual or regular (such as spending time with colleagues or friends or going to the office) — we switch to "automatic" and the new idea doesn't have a chance to embed itself in our mind.
- We haven't created a strong enough prompting mechanism to remind us of the idea at exactly the right time.

Wouldn't it be great if the solution to the problem was a massive billboard with flashing lights and loud music that magically appeared at just the right moment, with a reminder written on it in huge letters?

Although we may not be able to make a real billboard to do that, we can create the mental equivalent. First, though, it's important to understand about anchors and triggers.

TRIGGERS, ANCHORS AND THE SALIVATING DOGS

In a famous experiment carried out by Russian scientist Ivan Pavlov at the beginning of the last century, dogs were conditioned to associate the ringing of a bell with being fed. When dogs are about to be given food they salivate as the food is presented to them. What Pavlov discovered was that he could get the dogs to salivate without food, just by ringing the bell. Firmly **anchored** in the dogs' minds was the link between the food and the bell (achieved by conditioning). Once the bell was sounded, it **triggered** the salivation response even when there was no food.

Triggers and anchors work in humans, too, because over the years we've become conditioned to respond in certain ways to certain triggers. For example, if you're driving and you see a red stoplight, you'll automatically brake. If you're introduced to someone new at a social or business meeting and they offer their hand to shake yours, you'll automatically reach out to take their hand without even giving it a second thought.

TRIGGER	ANCHORED BEHAVIOUR
Red light	Stop the car
Offer of a handshake	Shake hands

APPLYING THE KNOWLEDGE

So, how can you apply this knowledge to ensure you always remember to do something at a particular time or place? It's quite straightforward – you simply create a visual reminder, which is anchored in your memory and automatically triggered by the specific event or place.

CREATING POWERFUL AUTOMATIC REMINDERS

Let's imagine you're going away on a trip and that the next time you catch up with your friend John you have to ask him if he'll take you to the airport in a couple of weeks' time. To do this, all you have to do is to follow the REMIND process:

Review in your mind what you have to do and imagine yourself doing it when you have to do it. Visualizing the action in this way will condition you to expect success. So, in this example, you'll envisage yourself asking John to take you to the airport when you see him next.

Exaggerate a picture of your trigger event (seeing John) and combine this with something related to what you have to do. You might see your friend sitting astride an airplane that was moving as if it were a mechanical bull. The more unusual and bizarre the image, the better. This is your anchored response.

Maximize the recall power of the image by using all your senses and the principles of effective memory visualization on pp.25–6.

Install the link firmly between your anchored response and the trigger by repeating the association in your mind a number of times so that every time you think of John, the picture of him sitting astride the airplane springs to mind.

Note whether the trigger will work or not by thinking of something else and then go back to thinking about John. If the first thing you think of is him and the airplane, the trigger's working. If it's not working, practise reinforcing it until it does, or find a stronger trigger.

Deepen the power of this process by affirming to yourself that it will work and that you'll remember by trusting your subconscious mind to remind you when you encounter your trigger (John).

What will happen when you next meet John is that seeing him will automatically trigger the picture of him sitting astride the airplane, which will remind you to ask him to take you to the airport. You've created your own mental billboard!

TRY THIS OUT

- To strengthen your understanding of this process, think of someone you know who'll benefit from this book and create a reminder to tell them about what you've learnt.
- Try out the REMIND process with something that you have to do at work or around the house.
- To convince yourself how powerful and long-lasting firmly anchored triggers can be, play some music from your teenage years and notice what memories come flooding back.

CHAPTER 3

GREAT TECHNIQUES

You're now going to discover a range of basic, easy-to-follow strategies for memorizing and recalling a variety of things from directions to spellings.

If you've ever forgotten someone's name within two minutes of meeting them, there's a good reason for it and this chapter will tell you what that is and how to deal with it. You'll also discover how to remember your PIN for your credit and debit cards and how to lock away, so you never forget them, those flashes of inspiration that seem to come at the most inopportune moment. You'll find out how to do your regular food shopping without a list and still remember to buy everything that you need. And you'll learn foolproof methods for remembering directions as well as for spelling troublesome words correctly.

REMEMBERING NAMES – THE SOCIAL METHOD

One of the biggest memory-related problems many people have is a difficulty in remembering names, which often leads them to think they have a poor memory. In most cases their memory is fine and the problem is just a matter of having an ineffective process for handling names.

WHY IS REMEMBERING NAMES SUCH A PROBLEM?

If I asked you to recall something you'd never been told, you'd think I was crazy. How can you possibly retrieve something from your memory that isn't there? Well, as silly as it may seem, this is the main reason why people have such a problem with remembering names – they never registered them in the first place!

For many, encountering new people at business or social functions is a stressful affair. With the pressures of wanting to create a good impression, the potential for rejection, the mental rehearsal of what you're going to say, the encounters with several people one after the other in quick succession and the myriad of other things swirling around your mind, someone else's name can hardly get through all that internal mental "noise" to stick in your memory.

THE SECRET OF REMEMBERING

What you need to dramatically improve your ability to remember people's names is a way to control the introductions so that you

definitely take in the names and remember them immediately.
The following process can be used in social or business situations.

REMEMBERING NAMES STEP BY STEP
Step 1 – Have your senses ready
When you're faced with meeting new people, you're going to learn something about someone, so you'll need to be ready to see the person's face and hear their name.

Step 2 – Shake hands
Address the person you're meeting by shaking their hand and saying hello. When you initiate the contact in this way, you can control the process and so are more likely to remember the name.

Step 3 – Name yourself slowly and clearly
This will help the person you're meeting to register your name but it will also mean they're likely to copy you and tell you their name in the same fashion, making it easier for you to hear and understand.

Step 4 – Concentrate
Do pay attention and concentrate when the person tells you their name by looking at their face and listening to what they say.

Step 5 – Say their name back
By doing this immediately, you definitely fix the name in your conscious awareness where it will be easier to remember.

Step 6 – Have you got it right?
Check with the person that you've pronounced the name correctly, and even check the spelling, if necessary, to clarify it. This way, you're starting a subtle process of repetition that will firmly engrave the name in your memory.

Step 7 – Ask about the name
By doing this, especially if it's an unusual name, you're continuing the process of repetition that will help you remember it, but you're also showing an interest in the person. This will create more of an emotional connection that will assist you in remembering them.

Step 8 – Keep the name in mind
Mentally review the name at every opportunity. Look around the room at the people you've met and silently name them to make sure you have their names in your memory.

Step 9 – Use the name
Employ the name at every appropriate opportunity, especially when you're talking to someone. "Janet, what do you think about this?," "That's an interesting point, Michael," "John, would you please pass me that glass?"

Step 10 – Exchange business cards
Say goodbye at the end of the function and exchange business cards if appropriate. Not only will this be a final repetition of the name but

when you receive the business card, you'll see the name written down and this will help you remember it.

Without this process most introductions between two people meeting for the first time are a one- to two-second rapid exchange of handshakes and barely registered names. And if you have to meet more than three or four people this way, it will be extremely difficult to remember their names at all.

KEEP PRACTISING

With practice, the introduction part of this process will take 15–20 seconds for each person that you meet. This will give you enough time to capture the name, repeat it a few times and develop a stronger connection with the person, which will definitely help you to remember them and their name.

As you go through the coming week, notice just how many people's names you already know. This will show you that you already have the ability to remember names. Also, monitor how many people you're introduced to in a week and notice how well you can remember their names following your old method.

Before you begin using the 10-step introduction process, practise it with friends or family members until you're comfortable with it and then use it the next time you meet someone for the first time. If you want to become really good at remembering names, you can increase the number of people you try out the process on by one more each time you use it.

REMEMBERING FACTS — THE MAGIC OF MNEMONICS

When you encounter a common fact, it's possible that someone has already created a simple and often clever way to remember it. Known as a mnemonic (pronounced **nem – on – ic**), such a device uses words as a memory prompt. Many mnemonics have been passed down through generations.

THE FIRST-LETTER METHOD

The most commonly used method for remembering information, especially when there's a set sequence to the data, is to take the first letter of each word you need to know. If you have difficulty remembering the colours of a rainbow, try this time-honoured device to help you recall them, based on the first letter of each colour:
Red Orange Yellow Green Blue Indigo Violet.

If we take the first letter of each colour, we get: R O Y G B I V

Many people remember the colours just by recalling "ROY G BIV", while others make up a sentence such as:

Richard Of York Gave Battle In Vain.

Whether you prefer the acronym or the sentence, you'll have a failsafe way to remember the order of the colours.

Another long-established mnemonic, learned by budding mathematicians, provides a simple way to remember a mathematical relationship: the trigonometric ratios of sine, cosine and tangent in a right-angled triangle in relation to the length of the hypotenuse and that of the sides adjacent to and opposite the angle in question.

Sine = Opposite/Hypotenuse
Cosine = Adjacent/Hypotenuse
Tangent = Opposite/Adjacent

To remember this mathematicians either use: SOH CAH TOA. Or a sentence such as:

Some Old Hag Caught A Hare Trying Out Artichokes.

Millions of children learned the names of the planets in our solar system, from nearest to farthest from the sun – Mercury, Venus, Earth, Mars, Jupiter, Saturn, Uranus, Neptune, and the former planet Pluto – based on a mnemonic using the first letter of each planet:

My Very Easy Method Just Speeds Up Naming Planets.

Another common mnemonic that uses first letters is HOMES, which acts as a reminder of the names of the Great Lakes:

Huron Ontario Michigan Erie Superior.

A MISCELLANY
OF MNEMONICS

Sometimes there are different ways to remember the same thing. For example, mariners need to know that port is left and starboard is right. Here are three options.

* * * * *

Notice there are four letters in the word PORT and the word LEFT.

or

Think of the sentence, "There's no PORT LEFT in the bottle because the sailors have drunk it all!"

or

Note the order in the alphabet of the initial letters of the words: Port comes before Starboard just as Left comes before Right.

* * *

From the sea to caves … In caves you'll see rock formations that hang down from the ceiling and reach up from the ground. These are called stalactites and stalagmites but how can you remember which is which?

STALAGMITE = GROUND   STALACTITE = CEILING

or

Stalagmites rise from the ground and stalactites drop from the ceiling.

"He who is not very strong in memory should not meddle with lying."

Michel de Montaigne (1533–92)

RHYMES AND WORDPLAY

Poems and rhymes can also help to recollect useful facts. One of the oldest examples is used to remember the year when Christopher Columbus landed in America:

"Columbus Sailed The Ocean Blue
In Fourteen Hundred And Ninety Two."

Using wordplay helps, too. Daylight Saving Time changes confuse many who do not know whether to put their clocks forward or back. Here's how to remember which it is:

Spring Forward, Fall Back

CREATING YOUR OWN MNEMONICS

When you're faced with new and maybe rather obscure facts, you may have to create your own mnemonics. Although the first-letter method is versatile, not everything can be broken down in this way, so try this next technique.

ASKING THE RIGHT QUESTIONS

Asking the right questions is a powerful tool to direct our thinking in a positive and productive way. The questions on page 60 are designed to stimulate your memory to create some powerful mnemonics. When you have to learn a new fact, quickly run through the questions – they'll generate lots of ideas to help you remember the information.

QUESTIONS TO ASK

First impressions
Is there anything obvious about this new fact?
What does this remind me of?
Does this look or sound like anything else more familiar?
Are there any patterns in the words?
What are the key words to summarize the main points?

*   *   *

Manipulate the fact
Can I break this down into manageable chunks?
Can I make this outrageous or bizarre?
Can I exaggerate this?
Can I make this colourful or funny?
Can I draw a picture to represent this?
Can I abbreviate any of the words?
Can I make a word from the letters of any words?
Can I make this rhyme with something?
Can I make up a poem or limerick?

*   *   *

Use comparisons
How is this different from other, related facts?
How is this the same as other, related facts?

*   *   *

Use your different learning styles
How can I make this **look** like something easy to remember?
How can I create a **sound** from this?
How can I create an **action** from this?

CHECK YOUR RECALL

Once you've come up with your mnemonic for whatever facts you're trying to remember, it's a good memory principle to check that you're able to recall what you've learnt by putting the information aside for a short time. Go and do something else to occupy your mind for 20 minutes, then come back to the information and prove to yourself that you really do know it. If there are any shortcomings in your recall and you find it difficult to recollect everything, work on the mnemonic to make it stronger, then test your recall again.

THINKING CREATIVELY

The beauty about trying to devise your own mnemonic is that, just by thinking about and around the information you're trying to remember in a creative way, you'll embed the facts more deeply in your memory, and therefore be more likely to retain them, even if you don't come up with an obvious mnemonic.

NOW IT'S YOUR TURN

Try creating your own mnemonic for the following fact – the size order from the largest to the smallest of the planets, which is:
Jupiter, Saturn, Uranus, Neptune, Earth, Venus, Mars, Mercury.

"When I was younger I could remember anything, whether it had happened or not."

Mark Twain (1835–1910)

REMEMBERING SPELLINGS

Spelling in English can be a challenge, because many words are not spelled as they are spoken. Often there are a number of ways to write the same sound. This can be confusing both to people learning English and to native speakers, but there are some tricks that can help you remember the correct way to spell words that are commonly misspelled.

USE YOUR EYES

If someone's poor at spelling, it doesn't necessarily mean they're not as intelligent as someone who's good at spelling. It's likely that they just have a poor process for recalling the order of the letters. Most poor spellers "say" the word to themselves and then spell it phonetically by interpreting the sounds into letters.

Good spellers do something different. When they want to spell a word, they tend to "see" the word in their mind's eye and then copy what they "see". Because many words are not spelled as they sound, this process is more successful than trying to spell what is heard.

HOW TO REMEMBER AWKWARD SPELLINGS

Another secret of remembering how to spell words that habitually cause you a problem is to focus on the part of the word that you have difficulty with and to think up either a phrase or an image that you can link to the word to reinforce the correct way to spell it. Here are some examples:

Separate or Seperate?	There's **a rat** in sep**arat**e
Necessary, Neccessary or Neccesary?	Necessary has one "C" and two "Ss" because it's necessary that a man's shirt has one Collar and two Sleeves
Stationary or Stationery?	Envelope is an example of station**e**ry and it begins with an "**e**"
Embarrass or Embarass?	When we emba**rr**ass someone they go **really red**

And for young children learning new words for the first time:

Because	**B**ig **e**lephants **c**an **a**lways **u**nderstand **s**mall **e**lephants
Wednesday	**We d**o **n**ot **e**at **s**weets **d**ay

These are just some of the more common and popular examples of how to remember spellings. The best ones, though, are those that you make up yourself as they are most likely to register in your mind. Try finding your own ways to help you remember these commonly misspelled words:

Fahrenheit (it shouldn't be Farenheit), **Desiccated** (not Dessicated), **Supersede** (not Supercede).

When you're trying to spell a word, visualize it and then write it out rather than just saying it to yourself.

ALWAYS REMEMBER YOUR PIN

Personal identification numbers protect your credit and debit cards from misuse but often keep them so secure that even you can't use them because you've forgotten the PIN! What you need is a way to memorize numbers that's easy to use, works every time and still maintains the security of all your cards.

CHOOSE A GOOD NUMBER

The beauty of this first simple method is that you're allowed to choose whatever number you want for your PIN. It makes sense not to select an obvious combination like 1234, 1111 or 2222. The best number to choose is one that's unique and personal to you, yet not too obvious. For example, you could choose the date of your mother's birthday, the year your eldest child was born, the year your favourite team last won the Super Bowl or World Series, or any other four-digit number that has a particular meaning or association for you.

Below are two things that you can then do to remember your PIN when you need it. See which suits you better.

- Create a vivid image that links the significant number you've chosen and your card. If you've chosen your mother's birthday for your Amex number, then imagine your mother using that card while wearing a party hat and carrying a birthday cake with lots of candles on it. When you get the card out, you'll think of your mother using it on her birthday and will then recall the PIN.

- Carry with your card a cryptic note, like "Buy Mom's birthday present with Amex." When you get that card out, just look at this piece of paper and you'll know the PIN – but the clue will be meaningless to anyone else.

Of course, you can adapt this system to any short number, such as debit cards, door security numbers or combination locks.

USE YOUR CREDIT CARD NUMBER

Another foolproof method of remembering your PIN is to choose one based on the credit card number itself. For example, suppose your card number was:

4929 4263 7812 3611

It would be unwise to pick one of these four digit groups or any easy-to-guess combination, but you could use it as a basis for your PIN by, for instance, taking the first number of each group and adding 1 to it, to give you 5584. Whatever method you choose, you can have a unique PIN that you'll be able to recall simply by looking at your card.

MIX AND MATCH

If you've just one card and one PIN to remember, choose the method you like best and use that. If you've more than one card, pick a unique PIN for each card and commit each number to memory using a different technique.

REMEMBERING DIRECTIONS

Getting hopelessly lost is something we'd all like to avoid, and asking for directions is a good way to prevent this from happening. However, having stopped to ask the way, many of us still end up in the middle of nowhere because we forgot the instructions we were given. Remembering directions can be straightforward with a simple system and a little understanding of how we think.

THINKING AND COMMUNICATING IN DIFFERENT WAYS

Of our five senses, what we see (visual), hear (auditory) and feel or do (kinesthetic) have the most impact on the way that we communicate and learn. You and every person you meet will use these senses, but not in equal measure because, of the three, there'll be a personal preference. That preference (or learning style) dictates the most effective format for you to learn something.

When it comes to receiving directions, a visually biased learner will prefer to look at a map or see the instructions written down. Those who have an auditory preference will happily listen to someone describe the route, while people with a strong kinesthetic bias would rather be taken and shown the way.

The challenge comes when someone from one learning style attempts to help someone from another learning style — for example, when someone who prefers to see a map or written instructions is given directions orally. While they'll understand what's being said, they're less likely to take it in, and consequently they'll find it more difficult to remember the directions.

Think about your own ideal learning style. When you know what this is, it becomes easier to follow and remember directions if they're given in your preferred format.

However, when stopping to ask the way in a strange place, we don't always have the luxury of being able to obtain directions in our preferred learning style, so what we need is an effective process to remember spoken directions.

THE PROBLEM WHEN ASKING FOR HELP

There are a number of factors that tend to work against us when we're receiving oral directions from someone else:

- Too much unfamiliar information given too quickly for us to understand and remember.
- Men usually want to know the waypoints of the journey – for example, crossroads, road junctions and stoplights – and what to do at each one. Women, on the other hand, generally feel it's also important to describe every major landmark or notable feature along the way, such as a church, cinema or school. A man will often be confused and frustrated by a woman giving him directions, and vice versa.
- Asking for directions can be a stressful experience, especially if you're already lost and feel uncomfortable asking strangers for help. And your memory won't be functioning at its best if you're feeling stressed.

YOUR PERSONALIZED DIRECTION FILING SYSTEM

Instructions on how to get anywhere consist almost entirely of directions (left, right, straight on) and waypoints and landmarks along the way. As a journey breaks down neatly into stages, the trick is to prepare memory pegs for each separate instruction. And because directions are about moving around, it's appropriate to use your body as locations for these pegs.

Most simple directions will rarely exceed seven stages, so you might use an ear, shoulder, elbow, wrist, hand, hip and thigh as suitable locations. Should you need them, you could continue using locations down to your feet and back up the other side of your body for more complex instructions. Precisely how to use these pegs is described below.

Next, create memorable images for left and right — perhaps a glowing golden **L**ion with a massive mane for **L**eft and a giant long-eared, bright pink **R**abbit for **R**ight. Practise conjuring up these images so that the association of lion with left and rabbit with right (or whatever you've chosen) becomes instantaneous.

ASKING FOR DIRECTIONS – STEP BY STEP

The following process will help you absorb and remember directions so that you won't get lost.

- When you stop and ask someone for directions, always ask them for the "easiest" route. By doing this, you're subtly guiding the person you're asking into giving you clear, straightforward directions that you're more likely to be able to follow.

- As the person describes the route, listen for just the waypoints and memorize them by placing bizarre images of them on the pegs of your body filing system in order.
- Repeat the waypoints back to the person, but this time ask them what you should do at each one. So, if you have to turn left, incorporate a lion into your waypoint image, and so on.
- Repeat the entire route back to make sure you've got it right, but this time ask what notable features you might expect to see along the way. Add those features to the images that you've conjured up for each stage of the journey.

By doing it this way you'll go through the directions three times, each time layering on a little more detail and checking that you've got it right. The other advantage of this system is that it will also give you the time you need to memorize the instructions properly.

RECALLING THE DIRECTIONS

To recall the journey, think about the pictures you've placed on each part of your body in turn. So, for example, if you think of your shoulder and on it you "see" an image of a crossroads being jumped on by a huge pink rabbit holding a burger, you'll know that when you reach the crossroads you'll have to turn right and on your way there you'll pass a fast-food outlet.

This process is more laborious to describe than to implement – try it out and see. It's good fun and, as with so many memory aids, becomes second nature with practice.

REMEMBERING ERRANDS AND SIMPLE LISTS

By writing down a list of errands on a sheet of paper, you're neglecting to keep your memory in good shape, and if you lost your list you'd probably miss doing something that could be important. What you need is an easy, fun method to remember the list – as a bonus this will help you keep your memory in excellent condition.

THE MAGICAL POWER OF STORIES

Long before computers and audio recording devices were invented, and even before paper and pen, stories were used to pass down the folklore and history of societies and cultures for generations, often spanning hundreds if not thousands of years.

As a device for remembering, stories are extremely powerful because they bring information alive in a way that's easy to recall. A good tale is engaging, interesting and enjoyable, has a flow and a sequence with many highlights, and evokes a strong emotional response – all of which make it memorable.

HOW TO CREATE A GOOD STORY

Here's the secret of creating a story to help you remember errands:

- Be clear about exactly what it is you're trying to remember.
- Apply the techniques for using your imagination on pages 25–6 to create outstanding mental images of each item on your list.

- Create strong and powerful links between each image in an amusing, interesting and even bizarre story, making sure that you exaggerate and embellish, and use all your senses.
- Mentally review your story a couple of times to ensure that you've got the flow and can recall the items on the list.

Imagine that you have to remember to do the following things:
- Feed the cat next door.
- Buy a newspaper.
- Get the exhaust changed on the car.
- Take back your library books.
- Make an appointment with the dentist.

The first thing to do is to create a starting image that you'll always use for your current errand list. For example, let's take the image of a notepad and pen (which is what you'd probably use anyway to write down your list if you weren't trying to memorize it).

THE TALE OF A CAT
Based on the methods described above, here's an example of what the story might be.

Imagine a huge **notepad** with a bright red cover magically floating in the air. Above it is a large royal blue fountain pen that's busy scribbling away. All of a sudden the pages of the notepad begin flicking over quickly as though there's a powerful rush of wind. As they do so you hear a loud screeching "meeeeeoooooooooow" as the **next door cat** comes flying out between the pages and lands head first in a yellow bowl of cat food that's sent flying in all directions. The cat looks up indignantly, its head covered in cat food. It winks at you and then from underneath its paw it produces a copy of today's **newspaper**, sits up, crosses its legs like a human being, puts on a large pair of glasses and begins reading the paper. As soon as it's finished reading, the cat takes the newspaper and begins to stuff it into the **exhaust** pipe of your car. You get in your car and start the engine, but all of a sudden your car backfires with a huge bang that sends the rolled-up newspaper flying into the air through the window of the **library**. It smashes into a huge bookshelf, sending it crashing to the floor with books spinning off in all directions. People try to run out of the library to get away from the mess, but first they have to have their teeth checked by a very tall **dentist** wearing a purple gown and with a flashlight strapped to her head.

Review the story in your mind a couple of times, leave it a few minutes and then see what you can recall. To remember your errands, think of the notepad and pen, which should trigger the rest of the story, and from that you'll be able to recollect exactly what you need to do. Once you're comfortable with it, use this method whenever you have to remember a short list of things to do.

PRACTISING THE METHOD

Get your "memory muscles" in shape by trying the following exercises.

EXERCISE 1

Spend a few minutes creating a story to link and remember the following list of random items:

Bottle of mineral water
Small dog
Diamond necklace
Fountain pen
Bicycle

Put this book aside for 10 minutes, then write down the list of words. Check your answers against the list above.

EXERCISE 2

Now create a story to remember this errand list:

- Go to the post office to send a parcel to your friend.
- Drop your best suit off at the cleaners.
- Go to the store to buy some milk.
- Stop at the nearest ATM to get some cash.
- Pick up your shoes from the shoe repair booth in the mall.

Leave this book for 20 minutes. Then test your recall by writing the list down, with the aid of the story, and check your answers.

I MUST REMEMBER TO ...

Sudden flashes of inspiration often come to us when we're least able to write them down – for example, when driving or in the shower. At the time they seem blindingly obvious but, frustratingly, when we try to recall them later, our memory is blank. With the help of a simple memory technique you'll always remember your brilliant ideas.

YOUR FIRST MEMORY FILING SYSTEM

We're going to create the mental equivalent of a piece of paper and pen that you'll always have with you. So, whenever one of these ideas comes to mind or if you suddenly realize there's something you must do at a later date, you can make a note of it for easy recall.

On page 17 we talked about your memory working like a mental filing cabinet. You're now going to create a series of mental files for remembering your flashes of inspiration. This is the first of many memory filing systems you'll use as you develop a powerful memory with the help of this book.

THE NUMBER RHYME SYSTEM

The easiest way to organize a filing system is to number the files. Our first system will consist of ten files numbered from one to ten, but, as we find it easier to think in pictures rather than numbers, we now have to turn those file numbers into images. The system is called the Number Rhyme System because we find pictures of objects that rhyme with the sound of each number. Here are the images that are most commonly used. However, if a picture doesn't work well for you, feel free to replace it with one of your own that does.

1	Sun		6	Sticks
2	Shoe		7	Heaven
3	Tree		8	Gate
4	Door		9	Wine
5	Hive		10	Hen

CREATING POWERFUL IMAGES

The secret of making this system work for you is to create strong and powerful images for each of these "peg" words by spicing them up using the suggestions on pages 25–6. For example, for the number 2 we use the picture of a shoe. If you see one of your own shoes, it won't be as memorable as seeing a six-foot-tall stiletto-heel shoe made of shiny red patent leather. The picture must be so real and memorable that you can even "smell" the new leather.

Take a few minutes to create strong memorable images for each of the pictures – really go to town and embellish them. When you've done that, go and do something else for 20 minutes and then come back, write down the numbers from one to 10 on a piece of paper, and see how many of your Number Rhyme System images you can recall. What you're aiming for is to get to the stage where, as soon as you think of the rhyming word for each number, you automatically think of the corresponding picture.

HOW TO USE THIS SYSTEM

Your first memory filing system is ready to use whenever you're unable to write things down. Imagine you're in the shower and you've a sudden flash of inspiration about a problem. Create a spiced-up, memorable image of your idea using your imagination, and link that image to a Number Rhyme System file.

For example, if your idea is to try a different tool on a particularly difficult job, visualize that tool being heated by the sun (the first of the peg-word images) until it's too hot to hold.

Once you've mentally grabbed hold of the idea by creating a mental picture and linking it to a file in your memory, you won't lose that idea. To remind yourself of it, think of your Number Rhyme images and see what comes to mind.

YOU CAN REMEMBER OTHER STUFF TOO!

You don't just have to use the Number Rhyme System for capturing ideas. You can use it for any list or sequence of items, even my (deliberately) random list of words in the box opposite: book, table, giraffe, T-shirt, apple pie, mouse mat, telephone, wallet, DVD player, asparagus.

The more you can embellish the associations by using the principles of effective visualization and therefore really "see" the pictures you create, the better. Come back to the book in 10 minutes and check how many of the words you can remember by thinking of your Number Rhyme image for each number and seeing what pictures come to mind.

1	Sun	Book	Imagine a massive fiery sun melting the pages of a green book.
2	Shoe	Table	See a large ladies' shoe firmly embedded in a wooden table.
3	Tree	Giraffe	Picture hundreds of giraffes eating the leaves of trees in a huge forest.
4	Door	T-shirt	Visualize a T-shirt strolling up to the door (as though worn by the Invisible Man) and slamming it shut.
5	Hive	Apple pie	See a swarm of bees flying out of a hive and landing on an apple pie, which they devour, licking their lips.
6	Sticks	Mouse mat	Imagine a pile of sharp sticks and each one is piercing a colourful mouse mat.
7	Heaven	Telephone	Hear the loud ringing of a large telephone and watch carefully as a beautiful angel dressed in white floats past and picks up the receiver to answer the call.
8	Gate	Wallet	Listen to the creaking of an old rusty gate as it opens. And see hanging on the gate a large leather wallet with dollar bills falling out as the gate swings open.
9	Wine	DVD player	Imagine the red wine from your glass is dripping onto the open disk tray of your DVD player, much to your concern.
10	Hen	Asparagus	See a fat hen with a huge green asparagus tip under each wing and one in its beak.

SHOPPING WITH THE ALPHABET

Using a written list for your groceries not only causes a problem if you lose it, but also means you're letting your "memory muscle" go flabby. By creating a foolproof memory filing system just for your shopping, you need never have to search for pen and paper again, and you'll increase both your mental agility and your powers of concentration.

DO YOU NEED A TECHNIQUE FOR YOUR SHOPPING LIST?

Look at this list for two minutes, put the book to one side and see how many items you can recall.

Toothpaste	Cheese	Tomatoes	Steak
Bananas	Pitta bread	Salmon	Burger buns
Tuna	Strawberries	Yogurt	Toilet paper
Cabbage	Burgers	Carrots	Rice
Pears	Shampoo	Broccoli	Soap
Milk	Loaf of bread	Pasta	
Cream	Bagels	Deodorant	

Although you were probably able to recall some of the items, I'd be surprised if you could recall them all – 10 items is a creditable first-time score. However, before I give you a technique to memorize your list, there's a straightforward step that you can take first to increase your powers of recall.

THE FIRST STEP – ORGANIZING YOUR LIST

Take a piece of paper and organize this same list into five different categories. You decide on the categories based on what's on the list. When you've done that, go and do something different for 10 minutes and then see how many items you can recall.

You were probably able to remember more from the list by organizing it than you were if you just tried to remember it in the random order in which it was originally written. Organizing data in this way is called "chunking" and relies on our memory's aptitude for remembering things that are linked together in some way.

Another principle at work here is that, by grouping the different things from your list into the categories that you choose, you think about the list on a deeper level than if you had merely read it through. As a result, you're more likely to remember what's on the list because you've invested more mental energy in it.

Here's how I would have organized the list.

HOUSEHOLD ITEMS	Shampoo, Soap, Toothpaste, Deodorant, Toilet paper
BAKERY	Loaf of bread, Pitta bread, Bagels, Burger buns Pasta, Rice
FRUIT AND VEGETABLES	Pears, Bananas, Strawberries, Broccoli, Cabbage Carrots, Tomatoes
MEAT AND FISH	Steak, Burgers, Tuna, Salmon
DAIRY	Milk, Cheese, Cream, Yogurt

Now we have to find a way to completely and accurately remember this list.

THE ALPHABET MEMORY FILING SYSTEM

In the previous section I introduced the Number Rhymes for your first memory filing system. You could use this for remembering your shopping list but you'd be limited to just 10 items. In the same way that you'd use different pieces of paper for different lists, we're going to use different memory systems for different applications. In this instance, I'm going to show you how to organize your memory files using the alphabet, which gives you 26 hooks to help you remember.

The secret to the success of this system is that, as soon as you think of a letter of the alphabet, an image should immediately spring to mind.

Some letters will naturally lend themselves to a particular image, while other letters will require a little more thought. Here are the images I use.

Acrobat	Horse	Orangutan	Vase
Bee	Impala	Panda	Window
Cat	Jester	Queen	X-ray machine
Dog	Kettle	Rose	Yak
Eagle	Lasso	Snake	Zulu warrior
Frog	Mouse	Tarantula	
Guitar	Net	Uniform	

Some of these words and their images may not work for you, so feel free to change them for ones that do — Google's image-search facility on the internet will help you find pictures for each of the words that you choose. Here's a simple way to fix them firmly in your mind.

Take 26 pieces of thin cardboard (about playing card size) and on one side write the letter as large as you can and on the other write the name of your chosen image. Shuffle the cards and then, with the letters facing you, go through the cards in turn, seeing how quickly you can bring the associated image to mind. Do this until it takes less than a second for each card.

USING THE ALPHABET SYSTEM

You can now use your Alphabet System to memorize your organized list. Here's how you might start with the first three items:

Acrobat	Shampoo	Picture your acrobat balancing on a pyramid of shampoo bottles.
Bee	Soap	See a bee flying onto a flower and rubbing it with scented soap to give it fragrance.
Cat	Toothpaste	Imagine a cat cleaning its teeth.

Work through the entire list by category, creating strong associations between each item and the next letter. Don't try to conveniently match up images and items, such as Carrots with Horse. This system works by running through your image alphabet and recalling what you've pegged there, so the more outlandish the association the better.

REMEMBERING WHAT YOU'VE HEARD

If you've ever found yourself struggling to recall something you've heard in a conversation, it's natural to assume your memory is at fault. However, it's likely that you either didn't hear the information properly in the first place or you don't have a good strategy for remembering it.

WHY YOU SOMETIMES FORGET

There are a number of reasons why you may have trouble recollecting what you've been told:

- If you're not concentrating enough on what you're listening to, your mind starts to wander, and so, although you might be looking at the person who's speaking to you, your conscious mind doesn't hear what's being said and will have no recall of it.
- If your preferred method of learning is more visual or kinesthetic, you're likely to find recalling what you've heard more difficult.
- If what you're being told is complicated or difficult, you might become overwhelmed and lose track, which will make it difficult to understand and remember the information.

PRACTICAL WAYS TO ENHANCE YOUR RECALL

If you want to remember more of what you've heard, try one or more of the following tactics:

- Use the Rapid Repeat method – simply repeat in your mind what's being said as you hear it. This will enable you to focus

your attention more keenly on what you're hearing and prevent
your mind from wandering off.

- At regular intervals in a conversation, repeat back to the speaker
  a summary of what you've heard so you can keep track of what's
  been said.
- Ask questions often if you don't understand what you're being told,
  or get the person to explain the information in a different way.
- If possible, take notes that identify key words or phrases.

IDENTIFYING KEY POINTS

Developing the skill of identifying key points is critical if you want
to remember what you're listening to. A good way to practise is to
listen to the radio, especially dramas, and identify the points as they
emerge. You'll find with practice that you can summarize much of
what's said just by picking out these "high points" of interest.

USING MEMORY TECHNIQUES

Once you're able to summarize information in this way, you can use
one of the memory filing systems to record the key points of anything
that you hear. I suggest that you create a couple of 20-stage journeys
(see pp.102–5) that you use specifically for taking mental notes
during a conversation. Then, as you identify a key point, create a
powerful image of that point and link it to one of your locations. You'll
find that, if you memorize 20 key points from a conversation, other
details that you haven't necessarily memorized will spring to mind,
thanks to the power of natural association and connection.

RETRIEVING THE PAST

Most people like to reminisce, but retrieving the past isn't easy if there are gaps in your recall. However, you can recover many of your memories by understanding how to trigger and build on them. The trick is to start with something that you can recall and then build up the detail around it until you've recreated the entire memory.

FIND A STARTING POINT

Imagine that each of your memories is stored behind a different locked door. Sometimes these doors are quite easy to open but often they remain locked and the memory stays hidden. However, all you need to unlock a door to gain access to your hidden memory is the right key which, in memory terms, is something related to or associated with what you're trying to remember.

A great way to find the key and start the recall is to gather any items you have from the time you're trying to remember. These may be photographs, old diaries, clothes, toys or any other memorabilia from that period. Examine them closely and see what sensations come to mind. In particular, when looking at photographs, observe the detail around the subject of the picture to see what else you can recall. It's also useful to listen to music from that era or look at contemporary books and newspapers to help generate related memories. If the thing you're looking at is not the actual key, it might trigger something else that will unlock your memory.

ASK YOURSELF QUESTIONS

If you don't have any memorabilia to stimulate your recall, sit quietly, close your eyes, relax and take yourself back to that time in your imagination, focusing on something you can recollect about what you're trying to retrieve. Your aim is to re-experience the event as fully as possible. Ask yourself these questions to help stimulate your sensory and emotional memories:

- What did I see?
- What did I hear?
- What did I smell?
- What did I touch?
- What did I taste?
- What did I feel?

UNLOCKING THE MEMORIES

Whichever method you use, you'll find that, as one tiny piece of detail springs to mind, it will spark off the recall of another, related detail, which will prompt yet another. These keys will unlock your memories of the event or place, and the memories will come flooding back.

"The senses of smell and taste, weaker but more enduring ... continue for a long time, like souls, to remember."

Marcel Proust (1871–1922)

INTERLUDE
THE AMAZING WORLD
OF MEMORY

If you've worked your way through the exercises so far in this book, your memory will already be developing to a greater extent than most people could possibly imagine. Take a breather from your efforts and enjoy some interesting tidbits about the world of memory achievement.

FAMOUS MEMORY MEN

People have long been fascinated by impressive memory feats, and over the years many expert practitioners of memory have become household names to their generation. At the beginning of the last century many famous magicians like Harry Houdini wowed their audiences with stunning feats of recall, but it was only when people like Harry Lorayne in the US and Leslie Welch in the UK started performing dedicated memory shows in the 1950s that memorization and recall skills really came to prominence.

One of Harry Lorayne's favourite demonstrations was to recall the names of his audience, and over his career it's reputed that he's memorized the names of well over one million people. Today the stars of the memory world are people like Kevin Trudeau and eight-times

World Memory Championship winner Dominic O'Brien, who, among other feats, has memorized all the answers to Trivial Pursuit!

Most of these "memory stars" have trained their memory using techniques and ideas that are centuries old, but there are also some famous "savants" – people with an extraordinary natural memory. One such individual is Kim Peek. Born in 1951, Kim began reading books when he was just 18 months old and has now read and memorized over 9,000. He reads a page in eight to ten seconds, by which time it's stored on his "mental hard drive" for recall at any point in the future. Kim's memory ability is all the more astonishing as he has a low IQ and an inability to button his clothes or deal with the chores of everyday life. Brain scans have detected structural abnormalities in his brain but not enough is yet known about them to understand their full impact on his memory.

THE WORLD MEMORY CHAMPIONSHIPS

In the 1990s a group of dedicated mnemonists led by Tony Buzan, one of the world's leading authorities on memory improvement, set up a competition to see who had the best memory. From humble beginnings this competition has grown to a truly international event, attracting competitors and extensive media interest from all over the world. In addition, many countries now hold their own national and regional championships, as the acceptance of memory as a sport continues to grow. The competition is like a decathlon for the brain because it's spread over 10 events that are a combination of speed and endurance, where challengers for the title must memorize decks of randomly ordered cards, numbers, names, lists and a poem.

WORLD RECORDS

The world championships have delivered an amazing series of records that continue to be broken year after year. Here are just some of the staggering memorizing feats that the champions have achieved:

- Order of playing cards in one shuffled deck – 31.16 seconds.
- Number of shuffled decks of cards in one hour – 27 (that's 1,404 individual playing cards).
- Number of random digits in five minutes – 333.
- Number of random digits in one hour – 1,949.

Not all world records are set at the world championships. For example, the mathematical number pi (3.14159 etc) has fascinated people for centuries. It's an infinite decimal number that never repeats in a pattern and is the "Mount Everest" of memory achievement. The world record for this was set by Akira Haraguchi, a Japanese mental health counsellor, who managed to memorize and then recite the number's first 83,431 decimal places.

MEMORIZING REALLY IS GOOD FOR YOUR BRAIN

Some of these world records may sound a little beyond your abilities at the moment, but don't be deterred. With the techniques you'll learn from this book, together with a little practice, you too could manage similar feats. But even if you're not interested in pursuing a career as a professional mnemonist, your brain will be getting a good workout if you apply the ideas and techniques that you've learnt here.

In 2002 I participated in a study carried out by the Institute of Neurology in London where they scanned the brains of memory experts, who used the techniques I've covered in this book, as they memorized. Not only did the experts outperform the control group, but also it was found that more of their brain was being engaged, in particular the hippocampus, the part that's responsible for transferring short-term memories into the long term. It's also the part that "lights up" when we think about something that we know well. All this shows that memorizing really is a good form of mental exercise!

CHAPTER 4

WINNING WORKOUTS

Now that you have some basic ideas under your belt and have seen how easy it is to dramatically improve what you can remember, it's time to build on these foundations to improve your memory further.

This chapter still uses the principles you've already become familiar with but it introduces some new and versatile techniques.

Here, among other topics, you'll encounter ways to remember a speech and not "dry up", as well as strategies for remembering what you've read – whether a newspaper article or a novel. You'll discover the trick of learning foreign vocabulary for easy recall, and of never forgetting another important date or appointment. You'll also be introduced to the most powerful of all known memory systems, which you'll be able to use right away to do some impressive memory feats.

REMEMBERING NAMES AND FACES – THE MNEMONIC METHOD

As well as the Social Method for remembering people's names, which I explained in the previous chapter, there's another technique that can be used in conjunction with it. Called the Mnemonic Method, this second technique employs memory principles to spice up a name and link it to a face, and vice versa, to make both unforgettable. It links in with Step 8 of the Social Method on pages 52–5.

YOU LOOK LIKE ...
One of the principles of memory is that we find it easier to remember things that are related or linked in some way to what we already know. How can we apply this when we initially meet someone?

First, find something in the person's appearance that instantly reminds you of something or someone you know. If nothing springs to mind, you'll have to exercise your imagination!

Try asking yourself (perhaps using a degree of creativity), does this person:
* Look like anyone I already know?
* Look like someone famous?
* Look like a typical XYZ (eg policeman, singer, lawyer)?
* Have any prominent features that make them instantly recognizable?
* Have any features I can exaggerate or caricature?

REINFORCING THE LINK

Once you've found a memorable image, reinforce the link by looking at the person and thinking simultaneously of the association. If you do this whenever you see that person again, your image link should automatically leap into your mind as a mental memory file. Practise finding strong image links by watching the news.

Let's assume you've met someone who instantly reminds you of the actress Jennifer Aniston (Rachel from *Friends*). Every time you see this person, your mind will be triggered to think of Jennifer Aniston, the associated image firmly anchored in your memory.

SEE PERSON > THINK OF JENNIFER ANISTON

REMEMBERING THE NAME

Next, you need to create hooks and associations to help you recall the person's name. The best way to do this is to convert the name into a picture and link it to the memory file of their face. Let's say that the person you've met is called Penelope Sanchez. To turn this name into a picture, break it down into first and second names.

Step 1 – Visualize the first name

Ask yourself these questions – you may not have answers to them all. Just focus on the ones that have striking and instantaneous answers.

- Is there someone I know called "Penelope"?
- Is there someone famous called "Penelope"? (eg the actress Penélope Cruz)

- Does "Penelope" instantly trigger a picture?
- Does "Penelope" have a meaning that I can turn into a picture?
- Can I break "Penelope" down into parts that I can turn into pictures? (Imagine a pen, eloping with its partner.)

I'll assume the image of Penélope Cruz is the strongest for you, so you now need to create a "memory-spiced" picture linking Jennifer Aniston (the person Penelope Sanchez reminds you of) to Penélope Cruz.

SEE PERSON	>	THINK OF JENNIFER ANISTON	>	THINK OF PENÉLOPE CRUZ

Step 2 – Visualize the second name

Ask yourself the same questions about the surname.

- Is there someone I know called "Sanchez"?
- Is there someone famous called "Sanchez"?
- Does "Sanchez" instantly trigger a picture?
- Does "Sanchez" have a meaning that I can turn into a picture?
- Can I break "Sanchez" down into different parts that I can turn into pictures? (Imagine chairs made of sand – "Sand Chairs" = Sanchez.)

Step 3 – Link the first- and second-name images

Let's take the image of "Sand Chairs" for the surname. You now need to create another strong and exaggerated link between your image of Penélope Cruz and chairs made of sand.

SEE PERSON > THINK OF > THINK OF > CHAIRS > PENELOPE
           JENNIFER   PENELOPE   MADE OF   SANCHEZ
           ANISTON   CRUZ   SAND

Your imagery might be something like this: you see the person you've just met and instantly she reminds you of Jennifer Aniston, which prompts you to think of Penélope Cruz standing on her shoulders. With a loud fanfare, Penélope jumps in the air doing a double somersault and lands on a large red chair that immediately turns to sand. Try out this technique with a few names until you've got the hang of it.

LINKING NAMES TO FACES

Observation is a key skill in memorizing, and another way to remember names is to link them to particular features of a person's face or physique, as in the two examples below.

Jane Field

furrowed brow like a furrowed field

creeper-like earrings and tan suggest Tarzan's Jane

Bill Wilson

He will soon (Wilson) lose all his hair

Bill = money – imagine dollar signs in his spectacles

REMEMBERING LONGER NUMBERS

Unfortunately, not all numbers are as short as a four-digit PIN for credit and debit cards. Longer numbers such as telephone numbers, membership numbers or bank account numbers can be particularly difficult to commit to memory and to recall. This section shows you ways to remember them whenever you need to.

WHY ARE LONGER NUMBERS SUCH A PROBLEM?

Lots of people have problems with numbers, so if you do, you're not alone. Some people just don't like them, often as a result of a bad experience in math lessons at school. Another reason is that the brain prefers to think in ideas, concepts and pictures – and although numbers can form part of those, on their own they can be easily confused because they are so similar.

People also have trouble with numbers in their raw numerical form because, as psychologists have discovered, the average person has a limited digit span – they can hold only five to 12 digits in their short-term working memory. The problem is compounded by the fact that their working memory has a limited time span – just long enough to receive a phone number and use it, after which the number fades swiftly away.

We'll look here at some simple but effective ways of memorizing longer numbers for a greater length of time, and later on I'll also show you some more sophisticated and complex techniques.

BREAK IT DOWN

On page 28 I explained that a principle of effective memory is to break things down, and this same principle applies to remembering longer numbers. A number such as the one below might be a little overwhelming:

9074365218

However, if you break it down in the following way, the number suddenly becomes less daunting and more manageable:

907   436   5218

Most people naturally pause between groups of digits when giving out their phone number, making the number much easier to deal with.

Now that you've broken the number down, there are various techniques you can use to turn the groups of digits into words and pictures to make them more memorable.

YOU'VE SEEN THIS IN ADVERTISING

I'm sure you've seen advertisements for companies where the telephone number is a mixture of words and numbers. A furniture store owner might implore you to call him on 1-800-9TABLES. This is easier to remember than 1-800-9822537 because "TABLES" has a meaning that you can visualize in your imagination. This word is derived from the telephone keypad, which allocates letters to numbers.

THE TELEPHONE KEYPAD

Using the keypad approach you can turn a number like 2446532668 into:

244 653 2668
BIG OLD BOOT

What words could you make out of the following number groups?

3475 344 8776 9882 4726 538 264

The only snag with this system is that sometimes the numbers don't give convenient letter groupings to make meaningful words. For example, 6218435792 gives the decidedly unmemorable "ma 1 vid kryb," among other equally meaningless variations. Also, there's no letter allocated to the numbers 1 or 0, so for any number that contains these digits, you'll have to use one of the following techniques.

NUMBERS = LETTERS

If the telephone pad system doesn't yield helpful words or images, you can use the Numbers = Letters System. All you do is to replace each number by a word that has the corresponding number of letters. For example, 1633 could become:

A Ginger Tom Cat or A Larger Red Rat

The beauty of this system is that you can start to choose words that are appropriate for the number of the person or service it belongs to. If, for example, part of the phone number for your hairdresser had the digits 4146, you could make up the phrase, "Only a Trim Please".

Using this method, make up your own memorable collection of words for the following sections of telephone numbers:

- 3396 – Doctor
- 7219 – Cinema
- 2754 – Plumber
- 1335 – School
- 2856 – Auto-body repair shop

THE NUMBER SHAPE SYSTEM

In chapter 3 I explained how to create a memory system using words that rhyme with the numbers from 1 to 10. Now I'm going to show you a system based on images of objects that look like the shape of those numbers. This system also includes an image for zero.

Learn the images (opposite) in the same way that you learned those for the Number Rhyme System (see pp.74–7). Embellish them so you can readily visualize them. Set them aside for 20 minutes and do something else. Then test your recall by writing down the numbers and their corresponding images, and see how many come to mind easily. Keep practising until the association and recall are automatic.

Once the associations are firmly embedded in your mind, you can use them to memorize any number, however long, linking each image in a vivid scenario. For example, the number 8167 could be represented by a giant, carrot-nosed snowman (8) taking a bright blue baseball bat (1) and whacking an elephant (6) on the backside who then scurries up to the top of a garish pink streetlight (7).

Try using this system to make up some images for the following numbers: 287, 435, 9815, 03461.

PUTTING IT ALL TOGETHER

Now you have three different methods for turning numbers into something more memorable, so when you're faced with a telephone number like 7652910843 for your doctor, just break it down and apply one or more of these techniques to remember the number. Try this with the number above yourself.

NUMBER SHAPE IMAGES

0 = Tennis ball

1 = Baseball bat

2 = Swan

3 = Pair of handcuffs

4 = Sailboat

5 = Hook

6 = Elephant's trunk

7 = Streetlight

8 = Snowman

9 = Balloon on a string

10 = Knife and a plate

THE JOURNEY TECHNIQUE

The oldest of all memory storage devices, the Journey Technique is also the most versatile, with numerous applications. In my opinion, it's the most powerful mental filing technique, too, as well as being easy to use.

HISTORY OF THE TECHNIQUE

In two of the defining civilizations of the Western world, that of the Romans and that of the Ancient Greeks, being a great orator was a sign of political power and influence. The ability to recite long passages from memory was an admired, even revered skill, the secret of which was the speaker's reliance on the Journey Technique.

In modern times the technique is still being used, and if ever you see anyone on television performing an impressive memory feat, it's highly likely they're using this method. In the World Memory Championships, the top competitors over the last few years have certainly used it – I did!

SO WHAT IS THIS AMAZING TECHNIQUE?

The principle of the Journey Technique is simple, and the reason the system is so powerful and easy to use is because it's based on places you're already familiar with. You create a mental filing system by taking somewhere you know well and picking various points on a journey around/through/in it. You then use those points as files or pegs on which to place what you have to remember, making sure you use strong links and lots of "memory spice". When you want to recall the information, you revisit your journey in your mind's eye and, if your associations are strong enough, as you pass each of your points you'll be reminded of what you put there.

You'll hear this system called the "Roman Room" system because the Romans tended to use a separate room for each location. It's also called the "Greek Loci" system because the Ancient Greeks preferred to use one room with various points (or loci) around the room on which to hang their associations.

It doesn't matter which way you do this as long as you can go to specific points or locations in the same sequence on a journey around an environment you can visualize in your mind's eye.

DESIGNING YOUR JOURNEY

The first step is to decide on a location for your first mental journey. I suggest you start with where you live and pick your favourite room. It's a good idea to physically go to the room when you're doing this, because that will create a more powerful journey than if you simply envisage it, but you can still achieve impressive results if you just think of somewhere you've been and know well.

The next step is to identify in the room a starting point for your journey. Pick something that's a defining feature: for example, in the living room it might be the bookcase, in the kitchen it might be the refrigerator. Once you've chosen your starting point, mentally walk around the room and identify nine more significant objects (the more permanent the better) in sequence.

If you were using your living room, you might have chosen the following items or waypoints from around your room:
1. Bookcase 2. Painting 3. Floor lamp 4. Window 5. Door 6. Dog bed 7. Chair 8. Small table 9. Sofa 10. Television

You now need to "condition" your journey in your mind, so it's firmly embedded. Close your eyes and mentally re-trace your route both forward and backward several times and see each waypoint as clearly as you can. This is a crucial step. Otherwise, a weak memory of your journey will result in poor recall.

USING THE JOURNEY TECHNIQUE
You can use this device to remember virtually any information simply by applying the principles we talked about in Chapter 1, notably the powers of imagination and association. The trick is to evoke a strong

image for each item that you want to remember and then link it in a vivid scenario to a stage on your journey. It's a good idea to have different journeys for different purposes – there's no limit to the number that you can create and use.

Try out the Journey Technique by picking a room in your house and designing a 10-stage journey. Then memorize the first 10 elements of the periodic table, which are:

- Hydrogen
- Helium
- Lithium
- Beryllium
- Boron
- Carbon
- Nitrogen
- Oxygen
- Fluorine
- Neon

While this may seem a bit daunting, think creatively about the words. What do they sound like or remind you of? For example, Beryllium = berry, Helium = heel, and so on.

SCIENTISTS HAVE PROVED IT WORKS!

I get very excited telling people about this particular technique because I know it works as a result of the amazing things I've been able to do with it. But don't just take my word for it. Medical researchers have proved it works, too, by scanning the brains of people who were using the technique and a control group who weren't. The researchers discovered that memory performance was better in the first group than in the second and that using the Journey Technique stimulated more of the hippocampus (an important part of the brain when it comes to memory) and the right side of the brain. I know this to be true because I was one of the subjects of this groundbreaking research.

REMEMBERING DATES AND APPOINTMENTS

Have you ever had to endure the embarrassment of forgetting the birthday or anniversary of a close friend or family member? Or missed an important appointment because it had completely slipped your mind? If so, by building on much of what I've shown you so far, this section will really help you.

REMEMBERING BIRTHDAYS AND ANNIVERSARIES

On page 43 I suggested you record important dates on your calendar, as it's good to have a written record of them. However, what would happen if you lost your calendar or temporarily mislaid it? Having all those important dates firmly installed in your memory so you can recall them easily would be really helpful.

This is the process for remembering these important dates:

THINK OF THE PERSON WHOSE BIRTHDAY IT IS	>	THINK OF AN IMAGE FOR THE OCCASION	>	THINK OF THE IMAGE FOR THE MONTH	>	THINK OF THE IMAGE FOR THE DAY	>	LINK THEM TOGETHER

As usual, you'll rely on a chain of strong associations that employ powerful visual imagery representative of the information that you've memorized.

CREATING PICTURES FOR THE MONTH

The simplest way to remember the months is to think of images that instantly remind you of each one. For example, when I think of December, I'm instantly reminded of Christmas and I see a jolly man in a red suit with a white beard. August is another easy one for me because it's vacation time and I picture my large colourful beach towel spread out on the sand. Here are the images I use, and if they work for you, by all means feel free to use them, but I suggest you try to come up with your own unique images because they'll be even more powerful for you:

January	A powerfully built American football quarterback – the Super Bowl takes place in January
February	A heart-shaped box of chocolates – Valentine's Day
March	A troop of soldiers marching
April	A large colourful umbrella – April showers
May	A tall May pole on a village green
June	A tank (the Normandy landings took place in June)
July	A billowing American Flag, because of Independence Day
August	A colourful beach towel
September	A student carrying lots of books going back to school after the summer vacation
October	An animated skeleton from Halloween
November	A plump Thanksgiving turkey with cranberry sauce on the side
December	Santa Claus

CREATING AN IMAGE FOR THE DAY

Next, create some pictures you can use to represent the day part of the date. For the dates 1–10 of the month, I suggest you use the Number Shape System (see pp.100–1) to conjure up images; for the rest of the days of the month, combine that method with the Number Rhyme System (see pp.74–7), as in the examples below.

In a two-digit number the Number Rhyme image represents the first digit and the Number Shape the second. Every date in the range 11–19 will always include a sun in the picture, every date between 20 and 29 will have a shoe, and 30 to 31 will have a tree, as in the examples below. (NS = Number Shape; NR = Number Rhyme)

2	Swan (NS)
8	Snowman (NS)
13	Sun (NR) shining on a pair of handcuffs (NS)
17	Sun (NR) shining down from a streetlight (NS)
25	Shoe (NR) being lifted by a hook (NS)
26	Shoe (NR) being worn by an elephant (NS)
31	Tree (NR) sprouting lots of baseball bats (NS)

Try this method out for yourself. Write down the numbers from 1 to 31 and create your own image for each number using the Number Rhyme and Number Shape systems. Then test yourself to see how easily you are able to recall the images. Keep practising until the associations are firmly embedded in your mind and you can recollect them instantly.

USING THIS SYSTEM

Now that you've done the groundwork, the rest is easy. Suppose you wanted to remember that your friend Julie's birthday was December 27, here's what you would create in your imagination:

PERSON >	OCCASION >	MONTH >	DAY
ENVISAGE YOUR FRIEND JULIE	CANDLES ON A BIRTHDAY CAKE	SANTA CLAUS (DECEMBER)	LARGE RED SHOE (2) AND A STREET-LIGHT (7)

You might see your friend Julie blowing out two huge green and red candles on a yellow birthday cake and, as each candle is extinguished, it's grabbed by a rotund Santa Claus who shouts out "Ho! Ho! Ho!" The candles magically turn into blue stilettos with streetlights for heels, and Santa Claus proceeds to put them on.

Whenever you think of your friend, you'll see this unusual picture – simply translate it back into the month and day. Have a go at devising your own visual scenarios for remembering the birthdays and anniversaries of friends and relatives.

REMEMBERING APPOINTMENTS

A failsafe way to remember appointments is to create a 31-stage journey that you use as your monthly "planner". For example, if you have an appointment at the dentist on the 16th of the month, link an image related to the dentist (a large pair of false teeth being cleaned by a six-foot toothbrush) to the 16th location of your journey.

LEARNING A NEW SKILL

Having a good memory isn't just limited to being able to recall facts and figures. It also plays a key part in learning and developing new physical and mental skills. When you're dealing with information, you can quickly get to the stage where you realize you either know it or you don't. Skill development is a more evolutionary process, which can be enhanced with a little inside knowledge.

HOW YOUR SKILLS EVOLVE

When you're learning a new skill, you go through a series of distinct phases in relation to your ability to perform that skill and the degree that you have to think about it as you do so. There are four key stages that you'll encounter in the acquisition of any new skill – from basics such as learning to cook or drive a car to learning to play a musical instrument or becoming a proficient first aider.

- **Unconsciously incompetent** – at this stage you're not aware that you don't know how to do something until it's pointed out to you, or you try something that you think you can do but can't. For example, as a child you probably weren't aware that you didn't know how to drive a car.
- **Consciously incompetent** – once you realize that you can't do something or aren't very good at it, you're consciously aware of your incompetence. At this point you (or maybe someone else) will decide that you need to develop this particular skill. You hit this

stage when you sat behind the wheel of a car for the first time and suddenly realized that, although your parents may have made it look easy, driving is, in fact, quite a complex operation involving a multitude of coordinated actions and thought processes.

- **Consciously competent** – after a period of training and development you're able to perform a task or activity but you still have to think about it. Remember when you were learning to drive a car – once you'd understood what the pedals and gear stick were for, you still had to think about how to use them to start with, particularly how to engage the different gears.

- **Unconsciously competent** – your skill becomes automatic so you don't have to think about it. If you've been able to drive for a while, you can probably hold conversations, listen to the radio, keep track of the other cars around you, and still do all that stuff with the steering wheel, pedals and gears that used to seem so difficult, without even thinking about it.

MAKING THE TRANSITION

Once you've reached conscious competence, it's just a matter of practice and repetition for the skill to become automatic and unconscious. However, making the leap between consciously incompetent and consciously competent, when you actually develop and acquire the skill, is the most important step, and it's at this point that many people falter and give up. The transition can be made much easier, though, by following a few of the simple techniques I've already explained in this book.

ENHANCING YOUR SKILL DEVELOPMENT
Be confident of success

One of the key sections of this book is "Being certain of success" (see pp.30–3) and everything I've outlined there will enhance your ability to develop any skill you choose. Here are the main points again just to remind you:

- Have a goal.
- Have a plan.
- Believe you can do it.
- Take action.
- Be positive.

Rehearse the skill in your mind

I've been encouraging you to use visualization techniques to create images in your mind's eye that are easy to remember. Visualization can also play an important part in skill development because the mind is unable to distinguish between a real and a vividly imagined event. If I started describing a succulent juicy lemon to you in great detail with its tangy citrus taste and bright yellow skin, the chances are you would begin salivating even though the lemon exists only in your mind. The reason you'd do so is because the body responds to the signals the mind gives it even if the mental stimulus is imaginary.

When you're learning a new skill, it's important to rehearse it in your imagination, because research has demonstrated that a thorough mental rehearsal boosts the skill acquisition process and is almost as good as real practice.

Visualize and store the instructions

Often, not being able to remember instructions on how to develop a new skill will hamper progress and cause frustration, making it easier to yield to the temptation to give up. The answer is to use a mental filing system in which to store these instructions – this will give you instant access to them whenever you want. I suggest you use the Journey Technique (see pp.102–5), and that you create a mental journey related to whatever skill you're learning.

For example, use the golf clubhouse as the setting for your journey if you're trying to improve your swing, or maybe the tennis club if you're seeking to develop your serve or backhand. Then simply place an image for each instruction at successive locations or waypoints on your journey. Whenever you need to refer to the instructions, mentally walk your journey to recall each one in turn. These instructions are only a temporary "crutch" to help you until the skill becomes automatic. Once you've become unconsciously competent, you won't need to refer to them any more.

FAILURE ISN'T FINAL

Probably the biggest factor affecting people's development as they embark on learning a new skill is the fear of failure. Getting something wrong is felt to be such a terrible thing that many people "freeze up" when trying something new (or maybe they don't even try it at all). What they don't realize is that failure is part of the learning process. Think back to when you last got something wrong or you failed. Did you learn a lot from the experience? If you want to double your rate of learning, you need to double your failure rate.

LEARNING FOREIGN VOCABULARY

International travel is much easier than it used to be, which means more of us are venturing abroad. To really experience and enjoy the countries and cultures we visit, it helps enormously to speak even a few words of the local language.

YOU DON'T NEED TO BE FLUENT TO GET BY

I find that many people who consider learning a new language are put off by the idea that they need to be fluent. Fluency in another language can be achieved, but it's not necessary in order to understand and be understood when communicating in another tongue. Studies have shown that even though languages have many thousands of words, most native speakers use a working vocabulary of only a few hundred.

LEARNING FOREIGN WORDS – STEP BY STEP

The process for learning foreign words is this:

- Take the word you want to learn in your new language.
- See if the word reminds you of something or be creative and find an association – the association doesn't have to have anything to do with what the word means at this stage.
- Take what the word reminds you of and link that to the meaning of the original word.
- "Condition" the association, practising it a couple of times to strengthen it in your memory.

This is how I'd go about remembering the meaning of a common German word.

- I'd focus on the target word, "Zimmer" (pronounced "tsimmer"), which in German means "room".
- "Zimmer" sounds like "simmer" so in this instance I see a simmering pan.
- I'd now create a crazy picture linking a simmering pan to a room (I'd use a house and visualize a pan in every room).
- I'd then condition the association chain from "Zimmer" > Simmering pan > Room.

Now when I hear the word "Zimmer" in German I immediately think of a simmering pan, which instantly brings to mind the bizarre picture involving one in every room of a house.

DEVELOPING A WORKING VOCABULARY

Once you get the hang of this method, you'll find that in about 10 minutes you'll be able to memorize at least 10 words so that they stick in your long-term memory. Over the space of three or four weeks you can develop a working vocabulary of any language you choose.

Initially, when you start using the language, you'll need to go through the process of thinking of your trigger words and the bizarre images to remind you of the translation, but very quickly, with continued use, you won't need to, because the words will have become part of your vocabulary in that language and you'll "just know" what they mean and be able to summon them up at will.

REMEMBERING SPEECHES AND JOKES

Public speaking is claimed to be people's number one fear.
If you have to give a speech and you're not used to public
speaking, it can be quite a daunting prospect. A major
contributor to the fear factor is the dread of drying up in
front of an audience and forgetting what to say.

WHY DO WE FORGET WHAT WE HAVE TO SAY?

If you recall from the earlier section on stress, when faced with a
threat or perceived threat, we go into a fight or flight response. The
body shuts down what it doesn't need to run away or tackle the threat,
and that includes part of the brain responsible for long-term memory.
Talking to a group of people can cause the fight or flight mechanism
to kick in if you're not sufficiently prepared, and the result can be
quite embarrassing as you struggle to remember what you have to say.

WHAT YOU CAN DO TO HELP REMEMBER YOUR SPEECH

The secret of being a successful public speaker, even if you're going to
give a one-time speech at your daughter's wedding, is quite simple:

KNOW WHAT YOU WANT TO SAY AND PRACTISE SAYING IT.

The crafting, organization and delivery of a good speech are outside
the scope of this book, so for our purposes I'll assume that you already
have your speech prepared. However, you'll find the process of putting

it together will give you an important level of familiarity with what you want to say, which will help your recall.

Step 1 – Break your speech down into sections
If you have a five-page speech to deliver, it's much easier if you break it down into 10 logical half-page sections. Spend a little time identifying the purpose of each part and give each a unique, but logically appropriate name.

Step 2 – Identify your main key words for each section
Under each of your headings choose key words that will trigger what you want to say in each section. For a half-page of writing you probably won't need more than three or four key words – you're looking for one for each idea or theme.

Step 3 – Practise delivering each section
Now that you have your sections and have identified a handful of key words for each, the next step is to practise delivering the sections, one at a time:

- Read the section out aloud so you get used to its rhythm, pace and message.
- Take the first key word and from memory recite the passage that it summarizes, focusing on the meaning rather than concentrating on repeating the passage verbatim.
- Check to see how accurately you recited what you've written. At this stage, expect to be able to recall only a small amount.

- Repeat the process for a maximum of three times until you're happy that you can recite what you need to for this key word, and then move on.
- Do the same with the rest of the key words.
- Once you've done this with all the key words for that section, try delivering the entire section just by looking at the key words. Do this three times only.
- Repeat the process for each section.

Most people will start with the first section and work their way to the end, but I've found I obtain my best results if I work backward from the last section to the first or do the sections in random order.

Step 4 – Practise delivering the whole speech
Using your list of section headings and key words as a guide, practise reciting your speech in its entirety, checking after each time against the full written version and making any necessary corrections. A good tip is to record your speech as you deliver it and then listen to it to identify where you can make improvements.

Step 5 – Memorize your speech
You'll find that by following the process of repeated recall that I've just described, your memory of what you need to say will be pretty good as it will be triggered by the key words in each section. Now all you need to do is to memorize the section names and the key words associated with each.

If you have 10 sections, I suggest you use a 10-stage journey (see the Journey Technique, pp.102–5) to remember their names. It helps to use an appropriate journey for the message (for example, a church for a wedding speech), but it's not essential. Conjure up a memorable image for each section title at each stage along the way.

Now memorize the key words for each section by linking them in a bizarre story and associating them with the image you've chosen for the section title. So when you walk around your mental journey, at each location you'll see an image for a section linked in a story to the key words associated with that section.

Step 6 – Practise your speech from memory
Work on your delivery by rehearsing your speech using your images as triggers. With enough practice you'll say what you need to without relying on your images – but they'll always be there if you need them.

THE ART OF REMEMBERING JOKES
If you've ever tried to tell a joke and forgotten the punch line, here's a simple way to remember it. You'll need a mental filing system in which to store your jokes – again, my own preference is the ever-versatile Journey Technique. Your first step is to develop a journey on which to place your jokes.

Next, create vivid images for the different parts of each joke and for the punch line and link them in a story to the stages of your journey. Practise recalling the images so they spring to mind effortlessly, then practise delivering the joke until you can do so confidently.

MIND MAPS®

For thousands of years the written word has been an effective mechanism for organizing, capturing and sharing ideas and thoughts. However, comparatively recent research into how the brain functions has identified that the tradition of just organizing words in a linear manner on paper may not be the best way to employ our cognitive abilities. There are other more powerful ways to organize our thoughts, and, in my opinion, the Mind Map® is the most effective.

WHAT ARE MIND MAPS®?

Mind Maps® present a diagrammatic overview of a topic, making it easy for the brain to assimilate the information. They were invented by British psychologist and thinking expert Tony Buzan in the early 1970s after his extensive research into memory and the most effective ways of organizing thoughts on paper for recall, problem solving and creativity. They engage both sides of the brain simultaneously – the left, analytical part and the right, imaginative, intuitive side.

Now used by millions of people around the world, the Mind Map® has been described as the ultimate thinking tool and is simple to use and easy to learn. The example opposite shows a basic Mind Map® incorporating the key features:

- A central image that represents the topic of the Mind Map®.
- A radiating structure of main key word branches that identify the themes of the topic.

- Smaller key word sub-branches that represent the detail of each theme.

A good Mind Map® will use the following:
- Many different colours to stimulate the right brain and allow distinctions to be made between themes and topics.
- Carefully chosen key words, preferably single and written clearly. Each one should sit neatly on a branch of corresponding size.
- As many images as possible (because pictures are the language of our thinking). Some sub-branches could simply have a picture against them and no words.

- Arrows showing associations between key words and their related images.

It's critical that the length of the branches matches the length of the words, because, when you come to recreate a Mind Map® from memory, one of the key features that you'll recall is size. For example, if you remember a long branch radiating off from the right, your mind will automatically look for a long word to go with it.

ADVANTAGES OF A MIND MAP®

If you need to remember information, especially over the long term, a Mind Map® is a powerful memory device. It's also an extremely effective tool for organizing your thoughts on paper — whether to plan out a report or record what you've read or heard. In fact, you'll find that you'll get far more out of these processes and improve your recall if you use a Mind Map® rather than writing things down, for the following reasons:

- You'll be using more of your brain and therefore bringing more of your powerful abilities to the task in hand.
- It takes much less time to create a Mind Map® than to write in longhand, and it's more enjoyable and engaging.
- The process of Mind Mapping® requires you to think about a topic in a more focused way than simply writing about it, thereby developing your cognitive abilities.
- It's much easier to edit and review information in Mind Map® form than longhand.

HOW TO DRAW YOUR OWN MIND MAP®

Creating a Mind Map® is a straightforward process. To start off, try this exercise based on a familiar topic – yourself!

*   *   *   *   *

Take a sheet of paper and turn it so that it's landscape format (longer side along the bottom).

*   *   *

Using at least three coloured pencils, draw an image of yourself in the middle of the page. Don't worry, you don't need to be good at drawing. You're not trying to achieve an exact likeness: the image is simply there as a starting point.

*   *   *

Think about all the important areas of your life and draw main branches from your central image to represent each one. Use a different colour of pencil for each branch. For example, you might have branches for your family, hobbies, work, friends, home and vacations – whatever's important to you. Write down key words or draw pictures for each main branch.

*   *   *

Draw smaller branches coming out from each main branch to add some detail about each topic area. Label each one with a key word and/or draw an appropriate image.

REMEMBERING WHAT YOU'VE READ

Among the most common experiences that make people think they have a bad memory, as well as forgetting names, is forgetting what they've read. It's a natural assumption to make, but one that's usually completely wrong.

WHY CAN'T I REMEMBER EVERYTHING I'VE READ?

Whenever I ask people to break down what they expect to happen when they read, I usually receive an answer like this:

Stage 1

"I expect to **see** characters on the page and **recognize** them as letters that form words that I'm then able to **read** and **understand**."

Stage 2

"I expect to be able to **remember** what I've read so I can **recall** it at a later date either to **use** myself or to **communicate** to someone else."

This is a completely reasonable set of expectations when you consider what you **want** from your reading but it's totally unreasonable when you look at what you're **doing** when you read.

Most people have only ever been taught Stage 1 (the reading bit), which is all they do, and don't bother doing anything to ensure that Stage 2 (the remembering bit) happens. So your expectations for the result you want are over-ambitious and exceed what you're doing to achieve that result. In order to remember more of what you've read, you have to actively do something with that information to ensure you **memorize** it.

Another reason why you sometimes can't recall what you've read is because you're distracted — your mind begins to wander and starts to think about other things even as your eyes are still reading the words. Because you're not concentrating properly on what you're reading, you're not consciously taking it in, and consequently you won't be able to recall it. This is why you often get to the bottom of the page of a book and can't remember anything.

BECOME A BETTER READER

The first thing I recommend you do is to become a more efficient reader. Going to school and learning to read is a wonderful thing but, unfortunately, the way most people have been taught to read sets up a series of poor habits that limit the speed we read at and creates an inefficient reading process. Here are a few ideas to help you become a better reader:

- Use a pencil (or your finger) as a guide as you read to stop your eyes jumping around the page (back-skipping to re-read words is unnecessary and slows you down).
- Rather than reading individual words, read in groups or clusters of words to take in meaningful chunks.
- Practise reading faster so that your mind doesn't have the opportunity to wander off and think of something else because it's so absorbed in your reading.

HELPFUL READING STRATEGIES

As well as improving your reading technique, you can also employ reading strategies for fiction and non-fiction that will enhance your recall by helping you become more engaged in the material.

- With non-fiction, quickly skim what you're about to read and preview it to identify where the "best bits" are so you can focus on them.
- Set yourself goals for what you want to glean in order to focus your attention.
- When you read, mark out key words and sentences with a pencil or highlighter pen.
- Take notes as you read to include your questions, observations and opinions.
- After you've finished reading, quickly scan through the material again to review what you've read.
- Finally, summarize what you've read in your mind to embed the information.

CAN I REMEMBER EVERYTHING?

The subconscious is extremely powerful, and there are those who believe that everything we've ever encountered in our entire lives is stored in the memory. However, it appears that most of these memories are accessible only via hypnosis (and even then there's doubt about whether memories accessed by this technique are, in fact, true memories). So, rather than attempting the impossible and trying to acquire the ability to recall absolutely everything that you read, you should aim instead to focus solely on what's important for you to remember.

BOOSTING YOUR RECALL

Just by becoming a better reader and using the strategies I've explained above, you'll find that you'll naturally be able to remember more of what you read. However, even with this improvement, you'll still need to memorize and condition the knowledge so that you can always recall it. Here are some ways to do so using techniques I've already told you about:

- Use a Mind Map® (see pp.120–3) to take notes as you read. You'll find that the process of using this powerful tool will focus your attention and encourage you to think more deeply about your reading material, ensuring that you're more engaged in it. You'll also have a memorable record of what you've read.
- Review your Mind Maps® regularly – after 10 minutes, a day, a week, a month, three months and six months to ensure the knowledge transfers to your long-term memory. At each review try to draw the maps from memory before checking with the originals.
- Take the key points from what you've read and use either the Story Technique (see pp.70–3) or the Journey Technique (see pp.102–5) to memorize them.

"It is certain that memory contains not only philosophy, but all the arts and all that appertains to the use of life."

Marcus Tullius Cicero (106–43BC)

CHAMPIONSHIP POINTS

With the skills you've developed by working your way through the proven techniques in this book, you're on the verge of being able to do jaw-dropping things with your memory. When you see those people on television performing amazing feats, such as remembering ridiculously long strings of numbers or multiple decks of shuffled playing cards, every one of them has been at the same stage in their memory development as you're at now.

You, too, have the ability to perform similar feats, and this chapter will show you some of the tricks of the trade used by memory experts who do these sorts of stunts. You'll be surprised how easy they really are.

Who knows, we might see you, after a bit of practice, on television or maybe doing exceptionally well in the World Memory Championships. (Don't laugh, because that's exactly what happened to me!)

THE MAJOR SYSTEM

Dating back to the 17th century, the Major System is a phonetic memory technique. Because of its sophistication and flexibility you can use it as a mental filing system or to remember numbers, dates and lists.

HOW IT WORKS

Numbers are coded to consonant sounds from which you can make words and then memorable images.

	SOUND	HOW TO REMEMBER
0	s, z, soft c (cereal)	"z" is the first letter of zero
1	The dental sounds – t, th, d	"t" has 1 down stroke
2	n	"n" has 2 down strokes
3	m	"m" has 3 down strokes
4	r	"r" is the last letter of "four"
5	l	"L" is the roman numeral for 50
6	The soft g or j sounds – g (gentle), j, ch (church), sh, dg (hedge)	In a mirror a handwritten 6 looks like the letter "j"
7	The hard g sounds – g (garage), c (crack), k, ch (charisma), ng (king)	With a bit of imagination the letter "k" is made up from a couple of 7s
8	f, v	When handwritten "f" has two loops like 8
9	p, b	In a mirror a "p" looks like 9

HOW TO APPLY THE SYSTEM

The Major System is straightforward to implement. All you have to do is to follow these three simple steps.

Step 1 – Allocate consonant sounds

Take the number you want to remember and then allocate the appropriate consonant sound to each digit. For example, the number 18374 would have the following sounds:

1	8	3	7	4
t, th, d	f, v	m	The hard g sounds – g, c, k, ch, ng	r

Step 2 – Make up a word

Pick a combination of the letters in the order of the numbers and add in vowels or the silent consonants "h", "w" and "y" to make a word or sequence of words. Remember, it's the sound of the consonants that's important. For example, 18374 could become the words:

Toffee Maker – t(**1**) f(**8**) m(**3**) k(**7**) r(**4**)

When you translate the numbers into words, you'll find that there's a range of possibilities. However, when you work back from the words to the numbers, there's only one combination of digits that "Toffee Maker" (or any of the other possible words or phrases) can be.

Step 3 – Embed the words in your memory

To fix the words (and therefore the number) in your mind, create an extravagant and unusual image to go with them. So if the number 18374 was the access code to your office building, simply conjure up a bizarre picture, which somehow associates the building with a toffee maker.

CREATE YOUR OWN NUMBER IMAGES

Now, with a bit of creativity, you can develop a filing system with a unique image for all the numbers from 1 to 100, or even beyond! Work on a few numbers at a time and commit them and their associated words and images to memory by practising the recall. You'll then have your own peg system for remembering long lists of items.

BEETHOVEN'S BIRTH DATE

How many times have you tried to remember historical dates or the dates of famous people but failed? The Major System is the perfect way to remember them.

Let's choose the number 1770, allocating the following letters 1=d, the first 7=g, the second 7=k and 0=s, which gives the words "Dog Kiss".

I'd then make a vivid image of a dog rushing up to someone and giving them a big sloppy wet kiss. But what use can that be? Well, if I tell you that Beethoven was born in 1770 and you take the image of Beethoven and link it with a dog giving him a big kiss, you've just used the technique to memorize the year of his birth.

You could have chosen the words "Tea Cakes" or "Duck Case". It really doesn't matter as long as the code is adhered to.

LEARNING FROM A CHAMPION

Like many of my colleagues who have carved out a career as a professional memory expert, I was inspired by eight-times World Memory Champion Dominic O'Brien. As well as being an impressive mnemonist, Dominic also invented his own memory system now used by thousands of people around the world.

THE DOMINIC SYSTEM

A simple but amazingly powerful concept, the Dominic System will allow you to remember any number of any length quickly and easily. It's based on assigning letters to numbers and then personalizing them by linking them to someone you know well — a family member or friend. You could also use a well-known figure or celebrity. All you have to do is follow these four straightforward steps.

Step 1 – Assign the letters to the digits 0–9:

0	1	2	3	4	5	6	7	8	9
O	A	B	C	D	E	S	G	H	N

Generally, "S" is used for 6 as the word "six" has a strong "s" sound, and "N" represents 9 as it's easier to use than the ninth letter of the alphabet, which is "I".

Step 2 – Create letter pairs

For the numbers 00 to 99, create letter pairs. Write them down on a sheet of paper. For example, 23 will have the letter pair BC and 10 will have the letter pair AO.

Step 3 – Think of a famous person

For each letter pair, find someone you know really well or think of a famous person with the same initials. For example, CD (34) could be Charles Dickens.

Step 4 – Pick a related object

For each person on the list identify an object that's related to them or that's typical of them in some way.

Here are some examples I use:

NUMBER	INITIALS	PERSON	OBJECT
48	DH	Damon Hill (Formula 1 champion)	Formula 1 racing car
37	CG	Craig Griffiths (a friend of mine)	Baseball bat (he's a big fan)

HOW TO USE THE SYSTEM

First, take the number you have to memorize and break it down into four-digit chunks. For example, 48379651 would become 4837 9651.

To remember the number 4837, take the person represented by the first digit pair (48) and link them to the object of the second digit pair (37). In my example I see Damon Hill dressed in his yellow racing overalls wielding an enormous, bright green, metal baseball bat.

Next choose a journey that you've created using the Journey Technique (see pp.102–5) to fix your number and its associated image in position. Repeat this for the second group of four digits.

To recall the number, mentally walk along your journey route and visualize the images you've created at each location. Translate the images back into the number. For example, when I see the image of Damon Hill and the baseball bat, all I do is translate it back to the number 4837. If I had to remember the number 3748 (same digit pairs but in reverse order), I would have created a picture of my friend Craig driving a Formula 1 racing car.

DEALING WITH ODD NUMBERS

Not all numbers break down conveniently into four-digit chunks – you may be left with one, two or three digits. To memorize these extra digits you can use a combination of systems.

One remaining digit: Choose the corresponding image from the Number Rhyme or Number Shape System (see pp.74–7 and 100–1).

Two remaining digits: Envisage the person represented by that number in the Dominic System.

Three remaining digits: Envisage the person represented in the Dominic System by the first two digits interacting with either a Number Rhyme or Number Shape image for the third digit.

REMEMBERING A DECK OF CARDS

One of the most impressive feats of memory is being able to recall the order of a shuffled deck of playing cards having only briefly seen each card once. With a little practice you too can do this either to impress your friends or become a winning player at the card table.

HAVE SOMEWHERE TO STORE YOUR CARD IMAGES

To start with you need a mental filing system in which to organize all 52 cards so you can recall them. I suggest you use the Journey Technique (see pp.102–5) because it's the most flexible and, to my mind, the most powerful system. Create a journey that has 26 stages so that when you memorize the cards you can link two cards to each location. I find that it helps to have three or four of these journeys so I can follow a fresh journey each time and avoid confusion.

CREATE UNIQUE IMAGES FOR EACH CARD

You now need to create a unique image for each card. You could start from scratch and design new images, but to save time and effort, I'd advise you to "borrow" some of the images that you've already assigned to numbers in either the Major System (see pp.130–2) or the Dominic System (see pp.133–5) – you can use whichever system you prefer. It's safe to do this as it's extremely unlikely that you'll have to remember numbers AND cards at the same time (I can say this from experience as I have never had to!).

ASSIGN A NUMBER TO EACH CARD

The first step in creating the images you need is to give each card its own number, based on its suit. For example, for clubs I use the numbers 10–22: (A=Ace, J=Jack, Q=Queen, K=King)

10	11	12	13	14	15	16	17	18	19	20	21	22
10♣	A♣	2♣	3♣	4♣	5♣	6♣	7♣	8♣	9♣	J♣	Q♣	K♣

For diamonds (30–42) the numbering would work like this:

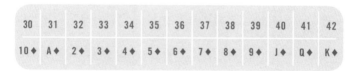

30	31	32	33	34	35	36	37	38	39	40	41	42
10♦	A♦	2♦	3♦	4♦	5♦	6♦	7♦	8♦	9♦	J♦	Q♦	K♦

I'd then do the same for Hearts (50–62) and Spades (70–82). Now link your Major or Dominic System image for the number 11 with the ace of clubs, the number 12 image with the two of clubs and so on. Then, when you're recalling the cards and you see your picture for the number 11, you know it represents the ace of clubs.

PRACTICE MAKES PERFECT

Practise converting each card to a number and visualizing the associated image. Then, link the images for pairs of cards together. (You're using a 26-stage journey so you'll need to double up images.) Finally, practise linking the doubled-up images to each location.

LONG LISTS OF SPECIALIZED ITEMS

Quizzes are extremely popular, particularly on television. If you want to pit your wits against the contestants, or just want to do better at a local quiz night, you can develop an encyclopedic knowledge of any topic using the techniques I've shown you in this book.

WHAT SORT OF THINGS COULD I REMEMBER?

Here are some examples of the question areas that may come up in a general knowledge quiz:

Kings and queens	Capital cities
Longest rivers	Roman emperors
US states and their capitals	UK prime ministers
Golf – US Masters winners	Constellations
US presidents	Currencies
Elements of the periodic table	Nobel Peace Prize winners

THE FIRST STEP

The most important step when preparing yourself to remember a long list of specialized items is to make sure that the information is correct in the first place. It's no good having perfect recall of an incredible list of facts if some of them are wrong. Once you've checked the information, there are two main techniques you can use to memorize and recall it.